Enterprise Leadership
The First Five FIELD Tools

ENTERPRISE LEADERSHIP
The First Five
FIELD TOOLS

Rick Mann, PhD
Dean Diehl, EdD

Enterprise Leadership: The First Five FIELD Tools
By Rick Mann, PhD and Dean Diehl, EdD

Published by: ClarionStrategy LLC, Nashville, TN

www.ClarionStrategy.com
www.ClarionToolBox.com

Copyright © 2022 Rick Mann, PhD

All Rights Reserved

Dedication

To Ken: who talked to a 29-year-old doctoral student
about "what could be."

Ken, not only have you been a remarkable enterprise leader
for 50+ years, but you have also inspired many others
to be enterprise leaders as well.

This book is for leaders and doctoral students
who aspire to enterprise leadership.

TABLE OF CONTENTS

Strategic Leaders Are Made, Not Born: The First Five Tools for Escaping the Tactical Tsunami by Rick Mann, PhD

Building Strategic Organizations: The First Five Tools of Strategy and Strategic Planning by Rick Mann, PhD

Strategic Finance for Strategic Leaders: The First Five Tools by Rick Mann, PhD and David Tarrant, MBA

Coaching: The First Five Tools for Strategic Leaders by Rick Mann, PhD

Leading Multicultural Teams: The First Five Tools for Global Leaders by Andrew Hoskins and Rick Mann, PhD

ACKNOWLEDGMENTS

Thanks to Trevecca Nazarene University.
This book was made possible, in part, by the leaders at Trevecca who granted me [Rick] a sabbatical to work on this topic and on this book. More specifically, my thanks to Dr. Dan Boone, the President of Trevecca; Dr. Tom Middendorf, the Provost; and Jim Hiatt, the Dean of the Skinner School of Business.

Thanks to our doctoral students.
As we have worked through these five FIELD topics over the last few years, I have greatly benefited from your insights. May you continue to sharpen your FIELD tools as you go forward.

Thanks to all the enterprise leaders with whom we have worked.
I have worked with many great enterprise leaders over the years. Your insights and engagement have been instrumental to the development of my own leadership theory and practice.

Thanks, from Rick to Cheri.
None of this would have happened without the support of my dear wife, Cheri. She is patient, kind, longsuffering, and I count it a privilege to be on life's adventure with her.

PREFACE

Welcome to the journey of enterprise leadership. Maybe you have been on this journey for decades, or perhaps this is all new for you. Regardless, my hope for you is that your experience with this material will be:

- **Clear** – Easy to grasp
- **Concise** – Short and to the point
- **Compelling** – Interesting and profitable

The purpose of this leadership book is different from others you might find. We are not trying to address all possible leadership topics. Instead, we focus on some key tools for those who want to lead at the enterprise level.

USE THIS MATERIAL EVERYWHERE

Our goal here is quite ambitious: We want to change your life. These concepts can be applied to your leadership and your organization, but perhaps more importantly, they can be applied to your personal life. They can be used everywhere.

Here, I am drawing on the McKinsey-Award-winning *Harvard Business Review* article by the late Clay Christensen, "How Will You Measure Your Life?" Christensen was a beloved professor at Harvard Business School and was voted the Best Management Thinker in the

World in 2011 (Thinkers50 awards are given every two years. Christensen was also #1 in 2013, #2 in 2015, and #3 in 2017). He is probably best known for his book *The Innovator's Dilemma*.

At its core, Christensen's article is about the importance of putting your personal life before your work life. To paraphrase his article, I can think of Dr. Christensen saying,

> At Harvard Business School, we teach the best and brightest from around the world. We teach them management, statistics, finance, strategy, and so on. Most of them will go into corporate life and be very successful. The problem is that some of them will be failures at home. This is a tragedy. I wish they could apply what they learn at home first and then in the corporate world.

Again, the above is my paraphrase and not Christensen's exact words.

I teach all of my graduate students and coach leaders with the same thing in mind. I hope that you can win at life first and then win in the workplace. Therefore, I use what I call the "PPO Approach." PPO refers to:

- Personal
- Professional
- Organizational

Whenever I introduce a concept, I give time and attention to how to apply it to your personal life, professional life, and organizational life. My family can tell you that I have often not done this well. However, with the lessons learned in my early adult life, I press on in this direction more and more as I get older.

THE GOLDEN CIRCLE

The Golden Circle was made popular by Simon Sinek, the author of *Start With Why*. As of 2022, Sinek's TED Talk on this subject has over 55 million views, making it the third-most viewed talk in history. In his work on this, Sinek talks about three circles: Why, How, and What. He expounds on **why** companies do what they do. He then discusses **how** companies do what they do. Lastly, he talks about **what** companies do. I have adapted this thinking for my work here. Each of the five tools listed in this book follows the same outline.

- **WHY It Matters** – Here, we look at why the tool matters. This includes the importance of understanding the concepts and putting them into practice. We also discuss why things may go poorly when the tool is neglected.
- **HOW It Works** – This is where we unpack the main concepts that are central to this tool.
- **WHAT to Do Next** – Here, we offer suggestions on what you can do next to put this tool to use in your personal life, professional life, and organizational life (PPO).

Enjoy the journey as you and others make your way toward greater enterprise leadership.

CURRENT THOUGHT AND PRACTICE LEADERS

Part of the value of this book and all those in the ClarionToolBox Series is that they incorporate key insights from thought and practice leaders and the hundreds if not thousands of pages of their work. Many of these leaders have been recognized by Thinkers50.com as the top management thinkers in the world over the past decade. A few of these include:

Clay Christensen (2011 #1, 2013 #1, 2015 #2, 2017 #3)
The Innovator's Dilemma (2013)
Michael Porter (2011 #5, 2015 #1, 2017 #5)
On Competition (2008)
Roger Martin (2017 #1, 2019, #2)
Playing to Win (2013)
The Design of Business (2009)
Rita McGrath (2019 #5)
Seeing Around Corners (2019)
Heidi Grant
Focus (2013)
9 Things Successful People Do Differently (2017)
Succeed (2011)
Carol Dweck
Mindset (2007)

NOTE: All of these authors and titles can be found in the Reference section at the end of this book. You can also find some valuable material in the Recommended Reading appendix.

Rick and Dean

As you read through this book, you can assume that Rick is writing unless Dean is noted. For example, if you read, "I was talking to a CEO one day," assume this is Rick narrating. If you read something like, "Innovation comes in many different forms [Dean]," then you will know it is Dean narrating.

INTRODUCTION

You Can Learn, Grow, and Change

On December 10, 2020, it finally hit me: Enterprise leaders are made, not born.

Dean Diehl and I were on a call discussing this book. As our conversation progressed, I realized three things for the first time. First, we had both started our careers out of college as public-school teachers. Second, we had both been MBA students later in life. Third, through education, developmental opportunities, and hard work, we had both become enterprise leaders.

When I wrote my first Clarion ToolBox Series book, *Strategic Leaders Are Made, Not Born: The First Five Tools for Escaping the Tactical Tsunami*, I wrote out of a conviction that anyone, even the most tactical person, could grow their strategic leadership.

When I started working on this book, however, I began with a more **fixed mindset** that some people were gifted to be enterprise leaders, while others were not. After the last few years of extensive work on this topic, my understanding of a **growth mindset** as developed by Carol Dweck (2006) has changed my thinking. I have finally concluded that enterprise leaders are also made, not born.

"Every high-performing organization needs several enterprise leaders," I said to the senior VP that I was coaching.

"Am I an enterprise leader?" the VP asked.

"Not yet, but you can be," I replied. "You'll need to build your financial acumen."

A growth mindset is woven throughout this book. If you want to grow as an enterprise leader, you can. What is your ultimate altitude? I don't know. Maybe you will lead a small company. Maybe you will become a corporate CEO. What I *do* know is that if you **learn** and **grow** in these five tools, you can **change** your altitude and realize more of your potential as an enterprise leader.

If you are leading at the enterprise level, your challenges will be greater and more difficult than if you were leading at a lower strategic altitude. Here are five ways in which enterprise leaders differ from the typical leaders we work with.

- **FOCUS**: Enterprise leaders see things more clearly, both up close and at a distance. They have an unusual **focus** that is bifocal in nature, which guides their life and work.
- **INNOVATION**: Enterprise leaders are marked by **innovation,** constantly seeking new ways to move forward in the value they create for their stakeholders.
- **ENTREPRENEURSHIP**: Enterprise leaders often find new markets and needs which can lead to starting endeavors to address these needs and opportunities.
- **LEARNING**: Enterprise leaders have a **relentless** desire to learn from others and the world around them.
- **DISCIPLINE**: Enterprise leaders have an unusual **discipline** that maintains their ongoing focus and drives all that they do.

While strategic leaders are in short supply, enterprise leaders are even less common. They are unusual, unique, and even "elite." While not all elite musicians, athletes, and other accomplished people are enterprise leaders, many of them share some of the same focus and discipline with enterprise leaders. In this book, we will explore how you can grow as an enterprise leader by developing these five tools.

While strategic leaders are in short supply, enterprise leaders are even less common.

What Is Enterprise Leadership?

In this book, we define enterprise leadership as follows:

Enterprise leaders bring insights, strategies, and skills to large or complex organizations that lead to effective performance that is sustainable and healthy.

As we unpack these 22 words, we see eight key concepts:

1. **Insights**: Enterprise leaders need cognitive frameworks that can guide their thinking and leading.
2. **Strategies**: It is not enough to have insights and vision. Enterprise leaders need mid-level strategies that can connect everyday work with higher-level priorities and vision.
3. **Skills:** Enterprise leaders need a bigger toolbox than lower-level strategic leaders. These strategies cover areas such as personal and professional self-care, team dynamics, process improvement, and strategic thinking.

4. **Large**: Most organizations get more complex and difficult to manage as they grow in scope and scale.
5. **Complex**: Some organizations may not have thousands of employees, but they are nonetheless complex in what they do. I once worked for a college president who said that a small college is like a nuclear power plant in that it has dozens of regulatory, compliance, and accreditation agencies to deal with.
6. **Effective Performance**: In this case, performance refers to reaching agreed-upon objectives for your department, division, or organization.
7. **Sustainable**: The goal here is high-performing enterprise leaders who can sustain effective performance not for months, but over years, if not decades.
8. **Healthy**: You can pick up almost any newspaper and see stories of leaders who have gone off the rails. In his book, *How Will You Measure Your Life*, Clay Christensen writes about his Harvard Business School classmate, Jeff Skilling, who went to jail because of his leadership in the Enron scandal. Our goal here is to develop healthy leaders, not toxic, dishonest ones. For more foundational material on this, refer to the Appendix in this book on the 5 Rs of Success, which includes being relational, responsible, resourceful, resilient, and realistic.

With these elements in view, we can frame the definition of enterprise leadership in the following way:

Enterprise leaders bring:

- Insights, Strategies, and Skills to
- Large or Complex Organizations that lead to
- Effective Performance that is
- Sustainable and Healthy.

Examples of Enterprise Leadership

The late leadership and management expert Peter Drucker wrote that, in his opinion, the four hardest jobs are:

- President of the United States
- College President
- Hospital CEO
- Senior or Lead Pastor

All of these roles have 24/7 responsibilities in complex environments. These individuals are not only responsible for leading and managing people, but also for inspiring and caring for those around them. People often ask me what it was like being a college president. I usually answer, "It was a lot like when I was a senior pastor. You are always doing some really meaningful things and you always have some people mad at you."

Not All Leaders in Enterprise Roles are Enterprise Leaders

In consulting and coaching with leaders and organizations, I have realized that some roles need enterprise leaders. Here are some examples:

- C-level leaders (CEO, COO, CIO, CMO, etc.) at for-profit companies and organizations with more than 100 employees
- C-level leaders at multi-national NGO (non-governmental or nonprofit organizations)
- School superintendents
- Governors
- As mentioned above: hospital CEOs, college and university presidents, and lead pastors at larger churches.

Just because a role needs an enterprise leader does not mean that there is one in place. I have seen many instances where an enterprise leader is needed for a role, but the role is being filled by a lower-altitude tactical leader.

Just because a role needs an enterprise leader does not mean that there is one in place.

Are Enterprise Leaders Born or Made?

Enterprise leaders possess a mix of natural-born attributes as well as a collection of developed strengths and skills. Keep in mind that the natural born characteristics that appear on the following list can always be developed further.

- Natural-born
  - Dedication
  - Ambition
  - Work ethic
  - Intelligence
  - Insight
  - High capacity

- Developed
  - Skills
  - Experience
  - Capacities
  - People skills
  - Grit
  - Resilience

It Is Not About Talent / Talent Is Overrated

As I mentioned earlier, enterprise leadership is not innate or fixed. It can be developed. This comes out of research and conviction that talent is overrated. In his book, fittingly entitled *Talent is Overrated*, Geoff Colvin quotes Anders Ericsson, a psychologist who has studied this topic for decades:

> **It is one of the most enduring and deep-seated of all beliefs about human nature—that natural talent plays a major role** in determining ability. This belief holds that some people are born with natural endowments that make it easier for them to become outstanding athletes or musicians or chess players or writers or mathematicians or whatever.
>
> My studies of experts point to quite a different explanation for why some people ultimately develop greater abilities in an area than others, with deliberate practice playing the starring role. So let's separate myth from reality by exploring the intertwined roles of talent and training in the development of extraordinary abilities. As we'll see, **innate characteristics play a much smaller—and much different—role than many people generally assume.**

What Ericsson and other researchers tell us is that talent is overrated, and that purposeful and deliberate practice are the secrets to high performance in many fields. In the same way, the attributes needed for enterprise leadership are not simply innate characteristics but rather a host of learned skills and practices.

On this topic, some people have said that Steph Curry, the all-star basketball player with the Golden State Warriors, has been one of the most transformational players in several decades. Why? Because he has inspired regular people to play basketball. People see that you don't have to be a superman like the 6'9" and 250-lb Lebron James. With extensive practice, average-sized people can become good basketball players.

Now when I say practice, we are talking hours and hours to be good at something. Those who would know say that Steph shoots 300-500 shots AFTER each practice. The moral of the story here, or based on research, is that with purposeful and deliberate practice, normal people can outpace talented people.

In my [Dean] experience in the music industry, the most talented musicians often fail as artists and as songwriters. Why? Extremely talented musicians often lack focus and discipline. People with a lot of natural talent get used to picking up new things easily and quickly. They can do almost anything and so they end up dabbling in everything.

Less talented musicians often have more focus and discipline because they only have a narrow range of ability, pushing them to concentrate on doing one thing really well as opposed to trying to do everything. Less talented musicians also have a lot of discipline because they have to work far harder than more talented people.

One of the most successful songwriters I know once told me he that wrote more than 200 songs over a 12-month period before landing his first song on a recording. I asked him what his life would have been like if his first song had been recorded. He immediately replied that it would have destroyed him. "Those 200 songs are what taught me to be a songwriter. If I hadn't had to go through that, I would never have developed the disciplined approach to writing that has made me so successful".

Strategic Leadership

A foundational starting point for enterprise leaders is to review the fundamentals of strategic leadership. These five tools are detailed in the Clarion ToolBox book *Strategic Leaders Are Made, Not Born* (2019).

- Creating Value
  - What do you provide that others value?
- Self-Awareness
  - How are you unique?

- Stakeholder Analysis
    - Whom do you serve?
- Strategic Altitude
    - At what altitude do you lead and work?
- Good-to-Great Rubric
    - Are you getting better?

Enterprise Leadership Is Not for Everyone

While many aspire to enterprise leadership, including those who want C-suite roles (e.g., CEO, COO, CFO, etc.), there is a price to be paid for leading at this level. Here are some examples:

- You must **work harder** than most others.
- You must be willing to **face regular pain and hardship**. Remember my earlier comment about how being a college president and being a pastor were similar? Both roles bring hardship.
- Even though they are around people all the time, enterprise leaders are often **lonely**. Many CEOs I have coached have no one at work with whom they can really be open and honest.

If you aspire to enterprise leadership, keep in mind that it may come with a fair amount of stress and strain.

Why Aspire to Become an Enterprise Leader?

If being an enterprise leader is so challenging, then why would you want to serve in this way? Here are some reasons:

- It Is **Interesting**: You are learning new things all the time. Life and work are not boring!
- It Is **Challenging**: Some people just like to take on challenges, whether climbing Mt. Everest, competing in the Olympics, or founding Tesla.

- It Is **Exciting**: If you like the high-stakes adrenaline of leading at a high level, you are in the right place.
- It **Pays** Better: Enterprise leaders are not common, and so they are often paid well, from the low six figures for nonprofit CEOs to the millions for some for-profit roles.
- It Provides **Social Standing:** People admire those who lead great things. I wouldn't choose this as your main reason for becoming an enterprise leader, but it is a side benefit.
- You Are **Called** to It: Many people just have to do it. They are called to lead all kinds of great endeavors.

Toxic Leadership

We all know leaders in enterprise roles who are toxic. Toxic leaders in enterprise roles often have the following features in higher proportions than others. They tend to:

- Focus on themselves.
- Have low self-awareness.
- Be slow to take feedback from others.
- Be quick to give feedback to others.
- Misunderstand the window and the mirror: they are more likely to look in the mirror when things go well and take the credit, and then look out the window and blame others when things don't go well.
- Tend to be in leadership for fame and fortune.
- Are slow to develop others around them.

We should all take time to self-reflect and consider our motives for enterprise leadership. Fame and fortune can be more alluring than we are willing to admit. Just be honest with yourself and with those close to you on your leadership motivation.

Foundations to Consider

As mentioned in the opening preface of this book, we don't know where you are in your journey. Regardless, here are three sets of resources you might want to consider as you begin reading this book: *5 Tools for Success*, *The Leadership Journey* (forthcoming in 2023), and other books in the Clarion Toolbox Series.

5 Rs for Success

In the appendix, you will find a discussion of the five Rs that are foundational for healthy leadership success at any level.

- Relational
- Responsible
- Resourceful
- Resilient
- Realistic

The Leadership Journey

Here, we describe five aspects of the journey from base camp to the summit.

- Character
- Work Ethic
- Toolbox
- Experience
- Credentials

Foundational Reading

If you have not already done so, we encourage you to read the following Clarion ToolBox books so you can better understand some of the foundational concepts. These books are inexpensive and can be read in an evening or weekend.

- ***Strategic Leaders Are Made, Not Born**: The First Five Tools for Escaping the Tactical Tsunami* by Rick Mann (2019)
- ***Building Strategic Organizations**: The First Five Tools of Strategy and Strategic Planning* by Rick Mann (2019)
- ***Strategic Finance for Strategic Leaders:** The First Five Tools* by Rick Mann and David Tarrant (2020)

NOTE: These are all available on Amazon.

Conclusion: Enterprise Leadership Is Essential for the Future

"Rick, what are your suggestions on who we should hire for this senior role?" the CEO of a large organization once asked me.

"You need an enterprise leader for this role," I answered. I then took a risk. "I don't think some of your other current senior leaders are enterprise leaders. Would you agree?" He responded affirmatively. I continued, "Knowing your organization well, my concern is that we cannot name 4-8 enterprise leaders in the entire organization." I paused. "My bigger concern is with what you are NOT doing to raise up the next group of enterprise leaders."

In most cases, I don't know your organization, but as organizations look to the future, they need to look at developing their pipeline of enterprise leaders. In their 2021 research report, entitled "CEOs For the Future: When the Future is Now," global consulting and talent management firm Korn Ferry writes:

> If CEOs are going to elevate their mindset to view the impact beyond the enterprise, they need **enterprise leaders** on their executive team. Whether the head of a business unit or a functional area, each leadership team member needs to bring a multidisciplinary point of view that can advance the thinking around the table, real or virtual. (p. 11)

As we conclude this introduction, we don't know if you are *a* senior leader or *THE* senior leader. Regardless, we want to challenge you to not only consider growing as an enterprise leader, but also how your organization can grow enterprise leaders.

There are needs everywhere. As Dean and I will attest, enterprise leadership is an exhilarating journey. If you are sensing this calling, these five tools may help. These tools won't make you an enterprise leader, but they can help you along the way. In review, each of the following chapters will work through these five FIELD tools:

- Focus
- Innovation
- Entrepreneurship
- Learning
- Discipline

We want to challenge you to not only consider growing as an enterprise leader, but also how your organization can grow enterprise leaders. There are needs everywhere.

1.

FOCUS:

Developing Bifocal Vision

The secret of change is to focus all of your energy, not fighting the old, but on building the new.

–Dan Millman

Focus like a laser, not a flashlight.

–Michael Jordan

"Rick, did you know that you have Shiny Object Syndrome (SOS)?" my coach asked.

"What does that mean?" I responded.

"It means that you are attracted to the next interesting thing," he continued. "If you don't address this, it is going to limit your senior leadership."

That was an important conversation. As I reflect on the past couple of decades, I realize that my leadership was not what it could have been. I too often lacked focus.

Some of this is related to my personality. On the Myers-Briggs Type Indicator (MBTI), I am an ENTP, which can be described as:

- The Visionary
- The Inventor
- Enterprising Explorer
- Debater

NOTE: ENTPs make up 3% of the population. Well-known ENTPs include Steve Jobs, Walt Disney, Thomas Edison, and Benjamin Franklin.

While I love the P side of my MBTI, which I describe as "the world of possibilities," it does lead to my SOS.

I, [Dean], on the other hand, am an INTJ. An INTJ is described as one who is, "Armed with powerful intellects and strategic minds, Architects (INTJs) can outmaneuver obstacles that seem unbeatable to most." (16 personalities.com, 2022). INTJs are also known as.

- The Mastermind
- Architect
- The Conceptual Planner

While I [Dean] am not as tempted to chase shiny objects, I have different traps to watch out for. For example, I love problem solving. In fact, I love it so much that I start to see everything as a problem to be solved. If there are no problems to solve, I have been accused of creating problems to solve. The point is, all of us, regardless of our personality type, have distractions that can keep us from the type of focus it takes to be an enterprise leader.

There is no perfect profile, but on the MBTI, the "Ps" tend to be more scattered than the "Js."

Regardless of your personality or profile, focus is essential for effective enterprise leaders. In this section, we will discuss **why** focus matters, **how** it works (with an emphasis on bi-focal vision), and **what** you can do next. Whether you are a strategic leader, an enterprise leader, or a graduate student, developing focus is critical to your success.

WHY IT MATTERS

Focus is one of the central factors that causes leaders and organizations to outperform their peers. Unfocused individuals tend to drift from one thing to another and have a hard time pushing through to sustained excellence. With my coaching and consulting clients, I observe a wide distribution of engagement. Some are focused on the process and find traction and growth. Others are adrift and often struggle with continued effectiveness. The same is true for our MBA and DBA students.

In their 2021 HBR article, "Every Leader Has Flaws. Don't Let Yours Derail your Strategy," Carucci and Lancefield write:

> The effects of a leader's personality on an organization's culture have been long understood. But we believe that some personality flaws have a disproportionately negative impact on the quality and execution of strategic choices — in particular, where to **focus**, how to compete, and what to build (and discard). (para. 3)

The reason we have selected focus as our first tool is because it is so foundational to all else that follows. Let's take a look at how focus works by unpacking SOS.

HOW IT WORKS

SOS

"You can't significantly change your organization's strategic focus every 90 days," I explained to the two senior leaders. I was serving their organization as a consultant and had been brought on to help them develop a strategy for their global work. I was wrong. They continued to change their focus every 90 days. The result was an unfortunate lack of traction and effectiveness which eventually led to the senior leaders' departure from the organization. Carucci and Lancefield (2021) continue in their article:

> Based on our combined 60 years of experience, we've identified four personality flaws of leaders and their specific impacts on strategy. (para. 5).

They go on to highlight four problem areas that some leaders face:

- The Overconfident, Chronically Certain Leader
- The Impulsive Leader
- The Rigidly Controlling Leader
- The Insecure Leader

With respect to the impulsive leader, they write:

> We've all seen the leader with "SOS." They can't resist the titillation of a new idea or the latest fad. They crave the adrenaline rush of pioneering what's not been done....This soon dies down once they catch on to the pattern of abandoning last week's big idea to pursue the next one. Instead, they wait it out, **unable to sustain focus on something long enough to see it through.** (para. 9)

Impulsive leaders struggle with SOS because they get distracted by the next idea. In a 2017 *Entrepreneur* article, "Do You Have 'Shiny Object' Syndrome? What It Is and How to Beat It," we read:

> At its core, Shiny Object Syndrome is a disease of distraction, and it affects entrepreneurs specifically because of the qualities that make them unique. Entrepreneurs tend to be highly motivated. They crave new technology and new developments.

And they aren't afraid to start new projects and create new things.

Ordinarily, these are great characteristics, but when SOS sets in, it forces you to chase project after project, and change after change, never settling with one option.

It's called SOS because it's the entrepreneurial equivalent of a small child chasing after shiny objects. Once they get there and see what the object is, they immediately lose interest and start chasing the next thing. For entrepreneurs, rather than literal shiny objects, SBOs may be business objectives, marketing strategies, clients or even other business ventures. (paras. 3-5)

Music artists are notorious for SOS. Most of the artists I [Dean] work with are easily bored and are constantly pushing to move between one genre and the next. Many artists, left to themselves, would put a country song, a rock song, a jazz combo, and a gospel track with full choir on the same album. Well, if you're Sting, you can get away with it, but most artists need to have laser focus on one genre if they are ever to get enough momentum to build a career. It seems I spend a huge amount of time and energy keeping my artists focused.

A middle school student who plays flute this year and trumpet next year is not going to get good at either. In the same way, if a student plays soccer this year and football next year, they are going to face limitations on their growth. When applied to leadership, we see that leaders in enterprise leadership roles will underperform if they do not address their SOS.

Leaders in enterprise leadership roles
will underperform if they
do not address their SOS.

The starting point of enterprise leadership is the ability and discipline to stay focused over time and avoid jumping from one thing to another.

The 2017 *Entrepreneur* article goes on to talk about what happens when SOS increases:

> - **Inability to finish projects.** Are you a better starter than finisher?
> - **Poorly planning your ideas and directives.** Inadequate due diligence or undisciplined planning follows SOS. This is when a person comes to a meeting and says, "I have an idea," but can't follow through on the details.
> - **Burning through cash.** When I do strategic planning with teams, sometimes someone will say to me, "Rick, this project is only a million dollars. Why do you want me to fill out this one-page project charter?"
> - **Confusing your staff.** When senior leaders jump around from idea to idea, it is confusing for those on the team. (para. 6)

NOTE: I have been guilty of all of the above. My hope is that you can avoid the many mistakes I (and those with whom I have consulted) have made.

In the next section, WHAT TO DO NEXT, we will provide some practical strategies for dealing with SOS.

Bifocal Vision

Bifocal vision is defined as "having lenses each with two parts with different focal lengths, one for **distant** vision and one for **near** vision." For enterprise leaders, bifocal vision is the ability and discipline to focus intently on the work in front of you as well as the larger work of your industry and even the world.

Steve Jobs was known for his insane attention to detail, including such seemingly minute details as the appearance of the inside of the computer case. He also had a long-range view of how computers would work in the world. Elon Musk has a similarly intense bifocal vision that allows him to obsess on near details as he also focuses on the larger world around him. Our hope here is that you can develop a focused and relentless bifocal vision.

A metaphor I like to use on this is a view of the Smoky Mountains, a large mountain range between me in Nashville, TN and my parents in Asheville, NC. I have stood on their porch and looked at the mountains many, many times, counting the ranges within sight. In the illustration below, you can see five ranges. I have counted as many as 12 at times. No matter how many ranges are in front of you, there are always trees in front of you as well as the distant horizon. Bifocal vision is the ability to focus on the trees as well as the horizon. One is your near focus, and the other is your distant focus. Enterprise leaders need both.

Let's work through the key aspects of focus, beginning with near vision before moving on to far vision.

Near Focus

To function well as an enterprise leader, you need to be good at the work in front of you. I had the opportunity to hear the acclaimed violinist, Itzhak Perlman, at the Schermerhorn Symphony in Nashville. I was amazed at how he had mastered his craft through years of focused effort. Enterprise leaders have the focus to master what is in front of them. They are good at what they do.

Using their near focus is often the starting point for enterprise leaders earlier in their careers. They get good at:

- Using their time well.
- Completing projects on time.
- Managing a team effectively.
- Dealing with crises as they arise.

These enterprise leaders have greater focus and intentionality than their peers. This is true of great athletes, scholars, musicians, and leaders. One of the reasons that organizations hire leaders with master's and doctoral degrees is because these degrees demonstrate an ability to focus on an extended challenge and see it through to the end.

In her 2016 book, *Grit: The Power of Passion and Perseverance*, researcher Angela Duckworth describes the obsessive focus of Hall of Fame pitcher Tom Seaver:

> The life Seaver described sounds grim. But that's not how Seaver saw things: "Pitching is what makes me happy. I've devoted my life to it….I've made up my mind what I want to do. I'm happy when I pitch well so I only do things that help me be happy." What I mean by passion is not just that you have something you care about. What I mean is that you care about **that same ultimate goal in an abiding, loyal, steady way.** You are not capricious. Each day, you wake up thinking of the questions you fell asleep thinking about. You are, in a sense, pointing

> in the same direction, ever eager to take even the smallest step forward than to take a step to the side, toward some other destination. At the extreme, **one might call your focus obsessive.** Most of your actions derive their significance from their allegiance to your ultimate concern, your life philosophy. You have your priorities in order. (Chapter 4)

I [Dean] have also been accused of obsessive focus throughout my career. I am notoriously bad at small talk and have a terrible habit of entering a conversation about sports, the latest news, or what people did over the weekend and flipping it over to an analysis of consumer behavior or the psychology of persuasion. I don't get invited to many parties.

When people ask me [Rick] what I do for fun, I tell them that I travel the world helping leaders and organizations to be more strategic. While I do like traveling (and my wife, Cheri, likes it even more), what I like even more is seeing leaders and organizations at their best. That is my passion and focus. It is why I wrote this book. Is this focus obsessive for me? Maybe.

When people ask me what I do for fun,
I tell them that I travel the world helping
leaders and organizations be more strategic.

Developing Expertise

What are you really good at? Where have you been able to focus your work and develop significant expertise? What do you think about that keeps you focused and disciplined? Enterprise leaders have that kind of focus. My good friend, Rick Melson, developed an early vision of becoming a college president. He came to me over a decade ago and asked for advice on that journey. We talked about his need to complete his doctoral degree. He spent five years doing just that. Next, he knew that college presidents did fundraising, and so he decided that he needed to do that well. He applied to my college to be a director level frontline fundraiser and didn't even get an interview because the VP said he didn't have enough fundraising experience. I encouraged him to press on, and he did. He went on to become the VP for Advancement (fundraising) at a small liberal arts college and then a comprehensive university. He raised over $130M in less than ten years. Yes, today in 2022, he is a university president. He was relentless in pursuing the near vision work in front of him as well as his distant vision of becoming a university president.

Distant Focus

While focus on what is in front of you is important, even critical, it is not enough. Enterprise leaders also need to focus on the bigger picture; the longer view. They need bifocal vision.

Distant focus is looking at the larger picture and the more distant horizon. Having grown up in an Air Force family, I have always had an interest in airplanes and spacecraft. I am amazed at how Elon Musk and his company SpaceX have been able to develop a booster rocket that can send a satellite into space and then come back down, landing on a platform tail first. This has been possible because of Musk's near focus on developing this guidance system technology and his distant focus on planetary exploration. He is truly an enterprise leader with bifocal vision. NOTE: Elon Musk was announced as *Time* magazine's 2022 Person of the Year. What is going on in your world, or in the world as a whole? To lead well at the enterprise level, you need to see the bigger picture.

Steve Jobs had an obsessive focus on fonts. Yes, fonts, the letters that you see in print or on a screen. In fact, the *DigitalTrends* website has an article entitled, "Steve Jobs: The Godfather of Fonts as We Know Them." Jobs first developed this interest during a calligraphy class he took as a freshman at Reed College.

At the time, computer screens could only display simple, mono-spaced, block letters. Jobs loved fonts and the beauty they could bring to publishing. He and his team at Apple spent thousands of hours getting their Macintosh prototype to display real fonts. Jobs' passion and focus on fonts changed the world.

> What Jobs did with the Macintosh was not just [to]revolutionize digital typography—that would have happened sooner or later. **The unique thing he brought to it was the democratization of digital type.**
>
> Phinney explains Jobs brought font menus to the masses, introducing not just experts but average consumers to individually designed lettering. "The idea that the average person on the street might have **a favorite font was a radical thing." (2011, paras. 6-7)**

Part of what enterprise leaders bring to their organizations is a bigger view of the world and their work. Some people say that Tesla is not a car company; it is a battery company. Some say that Amazon was never a book company, or a sales platform; it is a logistics company. Enterprise leaders see the bigger world and its implications for their work.

Distant focus is often about seeing beyond the obvious. When iTunes was first introduced, everyone thought the price point ($9.99 for an album/$0.99 for a single) was what was causing the recording industry so much pain. However, the real problem was the unbundling of the CD, which allowed consumers to buy one song at a time. I [Dean] quickly realized that it doesn't matter how much you are charging, when you go from selling 10 songs at a time to 1 song at a time, you've got a problem. Having the vision to see the true problem changes how you approach the solution. That is the value distant focus can provide: deeper insight into root causes versus a surface reaction to what first appears to be the problem.

Bifocal vision focuses on what is near as well as what is far. It can also be the focusing on what is inside and focusing on what is outside, as we explore next.

Bifocal Vision: An Inside/Outside Focus

This bifocal framework can also be extended to look at inside and outside issues as well. It is natural for most of us to look inside to our own work, our own team, or our own department. Enterprise leaders see the bigger picture across their organizations. In his 2021 *Forbes* article "Enterprise Leadership: New Leadership for a New World," Kevin Cashman talks about the five shifts needed in enterprise leadership.

- Move From Self to Service: It is not just about you, it is about the larger team.
- Think Across the Enterprise and Across the Ecosystems. It is not just about your team or department; it is about the larger organization.
- Practice the Meta-Mindsets of Courage, Purpose and Inclusion.
- Share and Develop Resources Across the Organization. It is not about getting more resources for your work, but rather sharing resources across the organization.
- Ask and Answer Four Big Enterprise Questions:
    - Purpose: The Big Why Question: *Why Is It So Important That We Exist?*
    - Vision: The Big What Question: *If We Lived Our Purpose, What Can We Become?*
    - Strategy: The Big How Question: *How Can We Get There?*
    - Talent: The Big Who Question: *Who Will Get Us There?* (para. 10)

We have talked about how bifocal vision relates to things that are near and far as well as inside and outside. Now let's look at how bifocal vision can be applied to inputs and outcomes.

A Focus on Outcomes Instead of Inputs

Most people, including leaders, tend to focus on inputs rather than outcomes. Inputs are the TEMP (Time, Energy, Money, and People) resources used to drive our work forward.

When I ask leaders, "How is it going?" many of them will respond, "We are working hard." Work is an investment of our limited TEMP resources. The goal is not to work hard. The goal is to advance our outcomes. If I asked you, "How is your garden doing?" and you answered, "We spent all day Saturday with the rototiller," that sounds exhausting, but it doesn't tell me anything about your garden. The goal of a garden is not to do more work, it is to produce a better crop of whatever you are growing.

I [Dean] like to think of outcomes in terms of destinations. While you need to "enjoy the journey," you can never lose sight of the destination. An enterprise leader always has at least part of their vision focused on where their organization is going and on how they define success.

For enterprise leaders, it is good to focus on both outcomes and inputs. Here is what that focus looks like:

- **Outcomes**: What do we care about most? What are our agreed upon outcomes and what are the data telling us?
- **Inputs**: What does our allocation of limited TEMP resources look like and how could we advance our outcomes even further with fewer inputs?

Persistence Over Time

Sometimes, people ask me how I completed my doctorate. I just tell them "I didn't quit. I didn't lose my focus." Most significant accomplishments take time. You don't get a master's or doctoral degree in a weekend. It takes focused persistence over months and months.

Focus is a tool that we need to develop for extended periods of time. The following example from the book, *Good to Great: Why Some Companies Make the Leap...And Others Don't,* provides an example of what happens when we lose focus.

Good to Great: Losing Focus

Jim Collins' 2001 book, *Good to Great*, uses the example of the famous leader of Chrysler, Lee Iacocca, to discuss how focused and disciplined leaders can lose their focus.

> About midway through his tenure... Iacocca, **seemed to lose his focus and the company began to decline again.** *The Wall Street Journal* wrote: "Mr. Iacocca headed the Statue of Liberty renovation, joined a congressional commission on budget reduction and wrote a second book." Worse than his moonlight career as a national hero, his lack of discipline to stay within the arenas in which Chrysler could be the best in the world led to a binge of highly undisciplined diversifications. (pp. 131-132)
>
> A great company is much more likely to die of indigestion from too much opportunity than starvation from too little. The challenge becomes not opportunity creation, but opportunity selection. (p. 136)
>
> The good-to-great companies appear boring and pedestrian looking in from the outside, but upon closer inspection, they're full of people who display extreme diligence and a stunning intensity. (p. 142)

Developing your focus over time is critical to success as an enterprise leader. Let's look at some next steps for putting these aspects of focus to use.

WHAT TO DO NEXT?

First, as you assess you own level of focus, you can begin by looking at your tendency to start well and to not finish as well. The *Entrepreneur* article on dealing with SOS provides some suggestions:

- **Sit on ideas before launching them.** Before you have your team begin work on that new project that's going to "change everything," take a moment. Do some more research on the idea and think about whether this is the best use of your company's resources. Not every idea should be acted upon, and giving yourself this "buffer time" can spare you from an overly hasty decision.
- **Communicate with your team.** When you have a new idea, talk to your team members about it. Ask them what they think and listen to their perspectives, concerns and needs. They'll be able to help you realize when you're moving too fast, and if you do decide to go through with your decision, they'll be happier that you came to them first.
- **Set both long- and short-term goals with each new project.** Slow down when you start to shift gears. Set long-term goals for every project, including how long you anticipate the project will last. Set short-term goals to help you close that gap and keep the team focused.
- **Abandon projects only when necessary.** Once your long-term goals are in place, don't abandon the project until you get there. The only exceptions would be if your project starts costing you far more money than anticipated, or the landscape has changed significantly enough to undermine the project's effectiveness entirely. (2017, paras. 10-12)

Systematically Review New Projects Across the Enterprise

Enterprise leaders often manage multiple divisions within a complex organization. A systematic review will help track how many new initiatives are occurring within the entire organization and allow prioritization and allocation of resources based on where momentum is occurring.

SOS does not have to plague your leadership for a lifetime. By growing your self-awareness and implementing new strategies, you can develop better sustained focus.

Developing Focus Habits

If you tend to not finish well, the good news is that you can develop new focus habits. When I was training for a 5K race, I hired a running coach. She told me to go out and run 30 minutes every other day for two weeks and not to let my heart rate go above 130. She added that I could walk if I needed to. At first, I thought her advice was dumb. Then I read Rich Roll's *Finding Ultra* (2013) where he tells his story as a former Stanford University swimmer who struggled with alcoholism. Roll decided to change his life and so he entered a triathlon competition. The problem was that he couldn't even finish. In despair, he hired a running coach who told him the same thing mine had told me: Go out and run slow for several weeks. For those of you who are curious as to how this training works, longer endurance running uses different parts of your body than speed activities. There is a good article on this in *LifeHacker* by Beth Skwarecki (2020) entitled, "You Need to Run Slower."

Becoming an enterprise leader (or a better enterprise leader) is about developing better habits. Many of my DBA students are 1) enterprise leaders in enterprise roles or 2) aspire to be enterprise leaders in enterprise roles. If you want to grow as an enterprise leader, you need to develop better habits, just like I did with my running. (NOTE: I achieved a personal best in my next 5K time after those training sessions).

If you want to improve your focus, clarify some goals you want to accomplish and drive them to the finish line. For example, in 2018, I set a goal to write a book for this ClarionToolBox series each year. Writing books is tedious work and it is easy to get tired of the topic, the research, the writing, and the editing. I have worked with several leaders on writing their own books and encouraged them not to lose heart and give up. NOTE: This is 2022 and this is the fifth book being written in this series. I am also excited as I see others taking up the challenge of writing their first book. Remember, here are some good habits to adopt to accomplish your goals:

- Clarify your goals in your mind.
- Write them down.
- Choose 1-3 rather than too many.
- Tell others (don't forget the social side of goal setting).
- Focus not on what you done, but on what you have left to complete (Halverson, 2012).

In working with leaders as grad students or coaching clients, I often find the easiest place for them to start is in these areas:

- Reaching and maintaining their weight goals (mine is always 169).
- Eating healthier
- Time management
- Finishing their MBA or DBA

These are easy areas to focus on (pun intended). Your growing focus skills can last you a lifetime and can be applied to endless areas of your life and work.

Consider Getting a Coach

Many high-performing people have coaches to help them function at their best. You can find a coach for work, for life, for health, and beyond. You may know that I am an ICF-certified coach. What you may not know is that I always have a coach myself. Why? For me, having a coach always brings more value than cost. More importantly, having a coach helps me become a better version of myself.

2.

INNOVATION:

Moving Toward Greater Value

There's a way to do it better—find it.

–Thomas Edison

Innovation is the ability
to see change as an opportunity—not a threat.
Innovation distinguishes between
a leader and a follower.

–Steve Jobs

As Dean Diehl likes to say, "If you are not innovating, you are dying." If creating value is at the heart of every great endeavor, innovation is about creating greater value for your stakeholders.

WHY IT MATTERS

These days, organizations and companies are moving faster than ever. If you continue to do what you have always done, you will be left behind.

Whether it is small-scale sustaining innovation or larger-scale disruptive innovation, or even innovative entrepreneurship, you, your team, and your organization (for-profit or nonprofit) need to be asking questions about how to engage your world more effectively.

Part of this journey involves looking at your strategy, and part of this journey involves looking at your culture. Either way, keep asking your team about innovation. When you do this regularly, you are choosing a better future.

HOW IT WORKS

Innovation is a broad topic with many meanings to different people. For example, there is an overlap between innovation and entrepreneurship. In this discussion, we will be looking at the pioneering work of Clay Christensen and others.

The late Harvard Business School professor Clay Christensen was for many years one of the leading voices on the topic of innovation. In this section, we will be drawing on his work and that of his colleagues:

- *The Innovator's Dilemma* (1997) by Christensen.
- *The Innovator's DNA* (2009) by Dyer, Gregersen, and Christensen.
- *The Innovator's Method: Bringing the Lean Start-up Into Your Organization* (2014) by Nathan Furr and Jeff Dyer.

Starting With an Outward Focus

Before we unpack the many nuances of innovation, we want to begin with this simple proposition: Innovation is about them, not about us. Innovation begins with an outward focus.

An outward focus is consistent with the fundamentals of value creation. Value is in the eye of the beholder. We don't decide what others value—they do. The purpose of innovation is to find ways to increase the way you and your organization create value for others.

Innovation is about them, not about us.
Innovation begins with an outward focus.

Different Kinds of Innovation

Innovation comes in several different forms. In the following pages, we will explore these three types of innovation:

- Sustaining Innovation
- Disruptive Innovation
- Innovative Entrepreneurship
- Sustaining Innovation

Christensen (1997) describes sustaining innovation as having these features:

> What all sustaining technologies have in common is that they **improve** the **performance** of **established** products, along the dimensions of performance that mainstream customers in major markets have historically valued.

Here are the critical concepts with sustaining innovation:

- **Improve the performance**: What does improvement look like with your current line of products and services?
- **Mainstream customers value**: What is it that your current customers value, and how can you add to that perceived value?

In his research on the music industry, Dean Diehl identified the introduction of digital downloads, most notably by Apple through the launch of its iTunes platform, as a sustaining innovation. Since their inception, the key competitive dimension of music playback platforms such as the LP, the Cassette, and the CD, was portability. Digital downloads improved on the portability of the CD by allowing consumers to carry the equivalent of hundreds of CDs on a digital player the size of a deck of cards. Because digital downloads improved along the key competitive dimension, they were a sustaining innovation as defined by Christensen.

Disruptive Innovation

Christensen (1997) contrasts sustaining innovation with disruptive innovation:

Disruptive technologies bring to a market **a very different value proposition** than had been available previously. Generally, disruptive technologies **underperform established products** in mainstream markets. But they have other features that a few fringe (and generally new) customers value. Products based on disruptive technologies are typically cheaper, simpler, smaller, and, frequently, more convenient to use.

Dean Diehl (2019) describes disruptive innovation in the following way:

> Simply stated, a disruptive innovation is one in which **the innovation's initial performance is considered to be inferior to existing options** in those attributes most valued by the mainstream market, called *core competitive dimensions*, leading mainstream consumers to dismiss the innovation. A disruptive innovation, however, survives because it finds a place among low-end consumers of the existing market or creates a new market due to its unique business model or its superiority to existing options in one or more attributes, called *secondary competitive dimensions*. **Over time, the innovation improves** its performance in the core competitive dimensions while maintaining its unique advantages **until**

> **it becomes acceptable to the mainstream,** allowing the innovation to encroach upon or *disrupt* existing options thus shifting the competitive landscape (Christensen, 1997; Schmidt & Druehl, 2008). (pp. 1-2)

Here are the critical concepts of disruptive innovation:

- **A very different value proposition:** Disruptive innovation changes the value proposition between the customer and what is provided.
- Disruptive technologies **underperform** established products: This is counter-intuitive but an important distinction with disruptive innovation.
- **Until it becomes acceptable to the mainstream:** Disruptive innovation takes time to become mainstream.

The Concept of Disruptive Innovation Has Evolved

Clay Christensen admits that over the years, the phrase "disruptive innovation" has been abused and updated. After 20 years (1995 to 2015), Christensen et al. (2015) wrote the following update.

> First, a quick recap of the idea: "Disruption" describes a process whereby a smaller company with fewer resources is able to successfully challenge established incumbent businesses. Specifically, as incumbents focus on improving their products and services for their most demanding (and usually most profitable) customers, they exceed the needs of some segments and ignore the needs of others. (para. 6)

Is Uber's Innovation Sustaining or Disruptive Innovation?

In their 2015 HBR article, "What is Disruptive Innovation?" Christensen et al. suggest that Uber is an example of **sustaining innovation** rather than disruptive innovation. They emphasize that Christensen's theory of disruptive innovation has two characteristics:

- Disruptive innovations originate in low-end or new-market footholds.
- Disruptive innovations don't catch on with mainstream customers until quality catches up to their standards. (p. 47)

Therefore, Christensen writes:

> Uber is clearly transforming the taxi business in the United States. But is it *disrupting* the taxi business?
>
> According to the theory, the answer is no. Uber's financial and strategic achievements do not qualify the company as genuinely disruptive—although the company is almost always described that way. Here are two reasons why the label doesn't fit. (p. 47)

Once again, Christensen differentiates sustaining innovation from disruptive innovation:

> Disruption theory differentiates disruptive innovations from what are called "sustaining innovations." The latter make good products better in the eyes of an incumbent's existing customers: the fifth blade in a razor, the clearer TV picture, better mobile phone reception. (p. 47)

Netflix as an Example of Disruptive Innovation

In contrast to Uber, Christensen highlights Netflix as disruptive innovation.

Netflix is a good example of disruptive innovation. Netflix was a disruptive innovation, not simply because it led to the bankruptcy of Blockbuster, but through the means by which it disrupted the video rental market. **Netflix found a fringe market that valued its online interface** and its subscription business model. It then innovated its way into the core of the market through improvement in the core competitive dimensions of convenience and selection. Most importantly, it shifted the existing market to a new subscription-based business model, which the established market tried, but could not imitate without destroying their existing value network. (Christensen et al., 2015)

While sustaining innovation and disruptive innovation are central to theories on innovation, there is also an overlap between innovation and entrepreneurship.

Innovative Entrepreneurship

While disruptive innovation can come from existing enterprises, it is more common to see disruptive innovation arise through the entrepreneurial efforts of new entrants. Yes, there is a link between innovation and entrepreneurship. The term used to describe this is "innovative entrepreneurship." This blend of innovation and entrepreneurship can be developed.

The Innovator's DNA

The discovery skills of innovation can be learned. On this, Dyer, Gregersen, and Christensen (2009) write in their HBR article, "The Innovator's DNA,"

> We found that innovative entrepreneurs (who are also CEOs) spend 50% more time on these discovery activities than do CEOs with no track record of innovation. Together these skills make up what we call the innovator's DNA. And the good news is, if you're not born with it, you can cultivate it. (p. 62).

Dyer et al. outline how innovative entrepreneurs have the following skills in higher amounts than others:

- Associating
- Questioning
- Observing
- Experimenting
- Networking

Let's look at each of these in more detail.

Associating

First, we have associating. On this topic of associating, Dyer and his co-authors write:

> Associating, or the ability to successfully connect seemingly unrelated questions, problems, or ideas from different fields, is central to the innovator's DNA. This associating will make more sense after we cover the next four. (2009, para. 10)

Questioning

Second, we have questioning. Here is what some of the top thinkers say about questioning. Peter Drucker says, "The important and difficult job is never to find the right answers, it is to find the right question." Ratan Tata of the Tata group says, "question the unquestionable." Lastly, Meg Whitman, former CEO of eBay and HP, says, "They get a kick out of screwing up the status quo" (Dyer et al., 2009, para. 14).

When I first came to Trevecca, one staff person said, "Rick, I have a nickname for you: Wave Maker. Whenever you are in a meeting, you like to make waves." That is probably true. While I try not to be irritating, I do see the value in asking the hard questions.

Observing

Third is observing. Innovators are constantly watching people around them. Scott Cook watched his wife struggle with keeping track of their finances. This led to the development of the innovative product, Quicken. If you listen to the podcast *How I Built This*, you will hear story after story about how innovators observed what was going on around them which in turn drove their innovations.

Experimenting

Fourth is experimenting. You don't have to be Thomas Edison, Michael Dell, or Steve Jobs to experiment. Over my years at Trevecca, the dean of the business school and I have discussed experimenting with our MBA program. First, we moved from on-campus to online. Next, we added data analytics, and then our MicroMBA. When I was asked about doing a MicroMBA, I said, "I am not sure how it will turn out, but I hope we continue to experiment with something new each year." Experimenting is part of the innovator's DNA.

Networking

Last, we have networking. Often, the best innovation doesn't come from talking to ourselves. Instead, it is as we get out and talk with others that we can come up with new innovations.
Let's review these five skills of the innovator's DNA.

1. Associating
2. Questioning
3. Observing
4. Experimenting
5. Networking

I [Dean] am known around Provident as the "Bumble Bee" due to my habit of never staying in my office but instead continually working my way from one office to the next serving as a catalyst for change. It is part of my role in helping the various divisions of Provident's somewhat complicated structure function as one company. I rarely bring about change myself but focus instead on getting the right people connected to each other for change to happen.

The Biggest Problem With Innovation Is You

If you want to move your work and organization forward through innovation, the place to start is with you. Yes, you and I are often the roadblocks to innovation because of our conventional thinking.

Let's take a detailed look the *HBR* article, "The Biggest Obstacle to Innovation? You." as to why many of us are limited in our innovative thinking.

> From even before kindergarten, we all were taught to reason in a way that works fantastically well in a predictable world: you establish a goal; you construct a number of plans to achieve that goal; you do tons of research to determine which is the best one; you gather the necessary resources to attain it; and you go out and execute on that superior plan.
>
> We think of this as prediction reasoning, a way of thinking based on the assumption that the future is going to be pretty much like the past.
>
> But when you are leading innovation, the world is anything but predictable. You are creating something that has never existed before and so you simply don't know how the world is going to react. By definition, innovation deals with the unknown.
>
> **And that's why you are the biggest problem when it comes to innovation.** If you keep using prediction reasoning in situations that are simply not predictable, you're bound to be disappointed and frustrated.
>
> You need a different way of thinking. (Schlesinger et al., 2012, para. 4)

Practice, Practice, Practice

One of the things I like most about Dyer's HBR article on the Innovator's DNA is the last section with the heading: "Practice, Practice, Practice." Yes, if you want to be an enterprise leader who leads innovation, you will need to practice. Dyer and his co-authors suggest, "spending 15 to 30 minutes each day writing down questions that challenge the status quo in your company" (2009, para. 30).

You don't have to be in an enterprise-level C-suite role to put these innovative practices to use. Each week, see if you can move one of these five practices forward in your world. Even better, have coffee with a co-worker and talk through these ideas.

Look Outside

We started this discussion on innovation with an emphasis on the need to look outside. While you can certainly look inside as one way to pursue innovation but that is often not the best. Kent Bowen, the scientist who founded CPS, an innovative maker of ceramic composite, is known for putting the following quotation on the wall:

> The insights required to solve many of our most challenging problems come from outside our industry and scientific field. We must aggressively and proudly incorporate into our work findings and advances which were not invented here. (Dyer, Gregersen, & Christensen, 2009, p. 66)

Design Thinking

Another aspect of innovation is design thinking which continues to grow in presence and popularity. IDEO founder David Kelley defines design thinking as:

> Design thinking is a human-centered approach to innovation that draws from the designer's toolkit to integrate the needs of people, the possibilities of technology, and the requirements for business success. (Turnali, 2015)

Tim Brown (2008) describes design thinkers as having the following attributes:

- Empathy
- Integrative Thinking
- Optimism
- Experimentalism
- Collaborations

In her 2018 HBR article, "Why Design Thinking Works," Jeanne Liedtka writes:

> I have seen that another social technology, design thinking, has the potential to do for innovation exactly what TQM did for manufacturing: unleash people's full creative energies, win their commitment, and radically improve processes. By now most executives have at least heard about design thinking's tools—ethnographic research, an emphasis on reframing problems and experimentation, the use of diverse teams, and so on—if not tried them. (para. 2)

For more on design thinking, you may want to read:

- "Design Thinking Comes of Age" (2015, HBR) by Jon Kolko
- "The Right Way to Lead Design Thinking" (2019, HBR) by Christian Bason and Robert Austin
- *The Design of Business* (2009) by Roger Martin
- *Change by Design* (2009) by Tim Brown

Innovation comes in a number of forms and is implemented by leaders in many different ways.

Forbes' Top 10 Most Innovative CEOs (2019)

As you think about innovation, you can also look to the following leaders who were ranked as the most innovative CEOs by *Forbes.*

- Jeff Bezos (Amazon) Tie
- Elon Musk (Tesla) Tie
- Mark Zuckerburg (Facebook)
- Marc Benioff (SalesForce)
- Reed Hastings (Netflix)
- Satya Nadella (Microsoft)
- Shantanu Narayen (Adobe)
- Tim Cook (Apple)
- Arne Sorenson (Marriot)
- Larry Page and Sergey Brin (Alphabet/Google)

Like all the tools in this book, innovation can be learned. You can grow in your ability to work and lead more innovatively. Let's look at some next steps.

WHAT TO DO NEXT?

The first step is to take ownership for innovation in your world. Make it *your* job, not a job for someone else. "For A.G. Lafley [Proctor and Gamble CEO], innovation is the central job of every leader, regardless of the place he or she occupies on the organizational chart" (Dyer et al., 2009, para. 29).

For A.G. Lafley [Proctor and Gamble CEO], innovation is the central job of every leader, regardless of the place he or she occupies on the organizational chart.

Ask yourself and those around you who is responsible for driving innovation in your team or organization.

Practice, Practice, Practice Today

As we mentioned above, innovation skills can be learned and developed through practice.

> The most important skill to practice is questioning. Asking "Why" and "Why Not" can help turbocharge the other discovery skills. Ask questions that both impose and eliminate constraints; this will help you see a problem or opportunity from a different angle. Try spending 15 to 30 minutes each day writing down 10 new questions that challenge the status quo in your company or industry.
>
> Innovative Entrepreneurship is not a genetic predisposition, it is an active endeavor. (Dyer, et al., 2009, para. 31)

Take action today and you can build your innovation skills as outlined in "The Innovator's DNA."

1. Associating
2. Questioning
3. Observing
4. Experimenting
5. Networking (Dyer et al., 2009)

Each month, review these five topics and see if you can move at least one of them forward. You can also spend time with your team, helping them to grow in innovation.

3.

ENTREPRENEURSHIP:

Pursuing New Opportunities

I'm convinced that about half of what separates the successful entrepreneurs from the non-successful ones is pure perseverance.

Being an entrepreneur is not about the money, or fame. It's about solving problems for society and the passion of creating opportunities where people only see problems.

–Steve Jobs

"Rick, could you start a Chinese language program in China?" To this day, I remember the moment I got that call and heard that question. *Why do we need another Chinese language program?,* I thought. There were already dozens of programs across Asia. As it turns out, however, there were several reasons to move this new opportunity forward.

First, while there are a seemingly endless variety of dialects and accents in the Chinese language, the most standard Chinese accent is found in northeast China. This Chinese accent is even better than that found in Beijing because Beijing has several local idioms. Therefore, we decided to set up the school in a major city in northeast China.

Second, Chinese language teachers tend to focus on reading and writing, while their American students want to focus more on speaking and listening. Therefore, we set up an innovative partnership with a local Chinese university and then built our own curriculum that focused on speaking and listening.

Thirdly, Chinese education is based more on rote memorization, which is not the best approach to modern language learning. Again, we innovated by developing our own curriculum and teaching methods.

Lastly, as I learned later, it is often good for beginning Chinese learners to have at least one teacher who is not a native speaker of Chinese, so that they can realize that this difficult language is not impossible for Americans. I started off as their first American teacher, but we added others later. I am happy to say that the program continued for two decades until it closed during the COVID era.

Entrepreneurship is about pursuing new opportunities that can add value for stakeholders.

WHY IT MATTERS

Products and services don't last forever—they tend to have a shelf life. In order to maintain or grow your market share and/or revenue, you need to add additional products and services. There are many nonprofits, for-profits, and social enterprises alike around the world that need new solutions.

Entrepreneurship is as much a mindset as an activity. Entrepreneurs are always thinking about how they can create things, solve problems, and reduce pain through new endeavors. Thus, today, there is an important role for entrepreneurial leaders and managers within existing organizations.

HOW IT WORKS

Howard Stevenson, "the godfather of entrepreneurship studies" at Harvard Business School, defines entrepreneurship as "the pursuit of opportunity beyond resources controlled." (Eisenmann, 2013, para. 2). Here, we see the pursuit of opportunity as central to entrepreneurship.

Dean Diehl and I define entrepreneurship as *"seeing the world through a lens of opportunity."*

Entrepreneurship is not just for those who want to start something from scratch. Entrepreneurial managers within existing organizations actively pursue opportunities around them and look for how their organizations might grow in different areas.

Entrepreneurship is seeing the world through a lens of opportunity.

Should You Look Inside or Outside? Maybe Both

While most people begin with an inside look at themselves and their organizations, most businesspeople start with an outside look. There are advantages to both. Entrepreneurs can benefit from adopting both an inside and an outside perspective.

Looking inside comes naturally when we think of entrepreneurship. This answers the question, "What do I want to do?" Most of us want to do what we want to do. Consider what you might want to move forward that could take your competencies and those of your team and transform them into new opportunities.

Looking outside begins by going out to markets and seeing what they want or need. This could be problems to solve and/or pain to address. For example, in the music business, Sony (Walkman, 1979) and Apple (iPod, 2001) created portable music players that allowed people to take their music with them.

Entrepreneurs can benefit from adopting both an inside and an outside perspective.

Job To Be Done (Milkshakes)

One of the iconic stories related to innovation and entrepreneurship comes from the late Clay Christensen. In his 2016 book, *Competing Against Luck*, he recounts a famous anecdote in which a fast-food restaurant chain hired a consultant to help them increase milkshake sales.

Christensen emphasizes that people do not buy products, they buy jobs to be done. They don't need drills, they need holes. As he explains, the job to be done by a milkshake in the morning is a different job than the one that needs to be done in the afternoon. In the morning, people bought milkshakes because they were neater than bagels and could keep them busy during their long commute. In the afternoon, parents often bought milkshakes as an after-school treat for their children.

As an entrepreneurial enterprise leader developing new products and services, you can begin by asking: What job do people need your product or service to do for them?

You can begin by asking: What job do people need your product or service to do for them?

The Lean Startup

If you read the book, *10 HBR Must Reads on Entrepreneurship and Start-ups*, you will see Steve Blank's article, "Why the Lean Startup Changes Everything." Here, Blank writes:

> Launching a new enterprise—whether it's a tech start-up, a small business, or an initiative within a large corporation—has always been a hit-or-miss proposition. As new research by Harvard Business School's Shikhar Ghosh shows, 75% of all start-ups fail.

> But recently an important countervailing force has emerged, one that can make the process of starting a company less risky. Although the methodology is just a few years old, its concepts—such as the "minimum viable product" and "pivoting"—have quickly taken root in the start-up world, and business schools have already begun adapting their curricula to teach them.

For years, I have taught the lean startup approach to our MBA and DBA students. Sometimes, I have students read Eric Ries' seminal work, *The Lean Startup: How Today's Entrepreneurs Use Continuous Innovation to Create Radically Successful Businesses.* I recommend this book to you as well.

At its core, the lean startup uses an iterative development cycle. Ries uses the above diagram to illustrate this cycle which begins with ideas that are built out into a product at first called a minimal viable product (MVP). Once a product is developed, the team then needs to measure the market response through data collection. The team must then finish with learning and then apply the lessons learned to the next iteration.

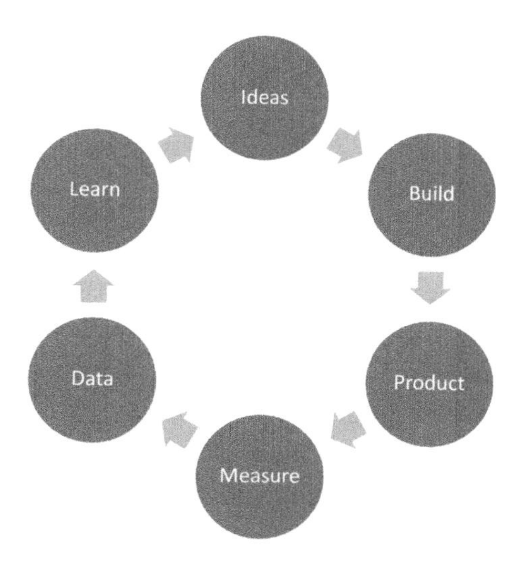

In my strategy consulting work, I have developed what I call the Strategy Cycle or Iterative Design Cycle (IDC). Both of these approaches have cycles that begin with developing an idea through strategic thinking and talking; planning and building a prototype or pilot; putting it into action; collecting data; and seeing what you can learn. Using these cycles allows you to make more progress faster with a lower investment of resources. When you take a long time and consume extensive resources, you run the risk of guessing wrongly what the market wants. An example of this was the Segway scooter, which proved to be a very expensive miss in the market. When you start off with shorter and simpler iterations, you learn quicker and can improve faster.

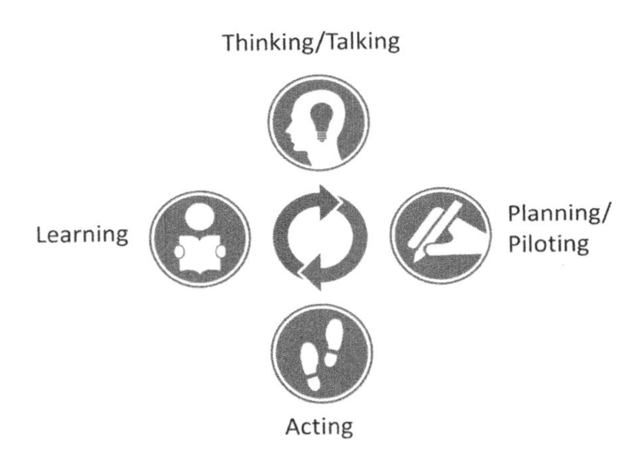

Putting Experiments Into Play

An extension of the lean startup is the use of experiments. In their HBR article, "Using Experiments to Launch New Products," Fossett (2018) and his co-authors lay out a simple experimental framework that can be implemented with new products and services.

Create a Hypothesis and Plan Your Data Collection: From the start, you want to develop a hypothesis that you can then test with your data. Michael Schrage (2014) defines a business hypothesis as follows:

> A business hypothesis is a testable belief about future value creation. It is not a search for truth or fundamental understanding; a business hypothesis suggests a possible or plausible causal relationship between a proposed action and an economically desirable outcome. If there is not an explicit and understood measure or metric for that new thing, it is not a testable business hypothesis. And if it isn't in writing, agreed upon, and shareable, it's not a business hypothesis. **Many good ideas fail on all counts above**. (para. 12)

A key concept here is "testable belief." For example, I could have the belief that people without a business degree do as well in our MBA program as those without a business degree. In that case, we are exploring "a testable belief" about future value creation.

Choose a Random Subset of Markets in Which to Launch: This allows you to take out differences found in just a single market.

Track Your New and Existing Product Data: You will want to see how much growth your new product adds and if it detracts from your other products.

Seek to Understand Why Success or Failure Happens: Your topline data and hypothesis are important, but you also don't want to miss other insights you might be able to gain.

Think about what experiments your team could run over the coming months. Try to introduce some experiments into your work each year.

Developing Entrepreneurial Leaders and Managers

The latest research shows that both leaders and managers need entrepreneurship. In the 2001 *Inc.* article, "What Makes a Good Entrepreneurial Manager? Ask Middle Managers," Gupta and MacMillan observe:

> As the rate of new technology development - and **the pace of competition - accelerate**, traditional approaches to management just aren't cutting it. Managers must operate in a highly

> unpredictable atmosphere in which competitive advantage may dissolve at any time. "**It's increasingly important for people to lead entrepreneurially**" (para. 3)

They go on to say that organizations that operate entrepreneurially are better able to:

- Gain first-mover advantage in new products or markets
- Provide a more fulfilling climate to employees, making it possible to acquire, develop and retain a talented, motivated human resource pool
- Succeed, through flexible resource deployment, in adapting capabilities to meet the emerging competition
- Effectively translate future options into a platform for continuous value creation and corporate transformation. (para. 6).

Four Features of Entrepreneurs

We naturally think of entrepreneurs as those charismatic individuals who strike out on their own to start something new. That said, we need enterprise leaders who can start new things where they are at. This could be a new product or service as well as a spin-off endeavor from your existing organization.

In Timothy Butler's 2017 HBR article, "Hiring an Entrepreneurial Leader," he talks about what he learned from interviewing over 5,000 entrepreneurs and general managers. Through this research, he uncovered four stereotypes we have about entrepreneurs. He then discusses the subtle truth about each of these four factors.

Creative: First, we tend to think of entrepreneurs as unusually creative. While this is true to some extent, the more foundational truth here is that entrepreneurial leaders are open to new experiences. They have an ongoing energy around exploring and learning. This is what enterprise leaders need: that desire to explore and discover what could be.

Risk: Second, another stereotype about entrepreneurs is that they seek risk. In fact, entrepreneurs do not seek risk—rather they are more comfortable than most with managing risk. When I was a college administrator in Minnesota, the local hospital's CEO came to me and asked if we could start a nursing program. I told them that this was a multi-million-dollar endeavor. After many months of discussions and research, I became comfortable that we could secure the funding sources and that good enrollment was probable. It only took three years before the program was the third largest at the college. We all knew there would be risk involved in this new large, entrepreneurial endeavor, but we figured out ways to manage the risk, such as doing our due diligence to line up partners.

Ambitious: Third, there is a misconception that entrepreneurs are more ambitious than others. The closer truth is that entrepreneurs like to take ownership of their projects. They also tend to be hands-on in their work. This does not mean that entrepreneurs exert top-down power. Instead, they like being in the middle of the action. Some years ago, I heard that Trevecca wanted to start a DBA program. I was a part of some meetings but was not too involved as there was already a new director in place. Sometime later, I asked the dean what happened to the DBA idea. He explained that it was on the shelf for now. After giving it some thought, I went to the Dean and AVP and told them I would like to try to get the DBA program up and running. Once I got into the action, the excitement of starting something new got my interest and energy up and going.

Salespeople: Fourth and lastly, the last stereotype mentioned in Butler's article is that entrepreneurs are natural salespeople. Based on his research, this stereotype is true. Entrepreneurs are active salespeople when it comes to promoting their projects. When I was working on a book on nonprofit leadership and management, I was looking for a case study that we could use in the book and our new MBA course on the topic. I asked our son, Jeremy, if we could use The Field School as our case study. The Field School is an inner-city elementary school in Chicago that is characterized as classical, Christian, and diverse. As a part of this case study, I conducted 14 Zoom interviews with Jeremy, the founder and Head of School for the Field School. As I listened, I realized that Jeremy had had to promote the school to many stakeholders. First, he had to sell the idea to a group of founding staff. Second, he had to sell the idea to donors who would help to provide the funding. Lastly, he had to sell the idea to the families of prospective students. If you want to start a new endeavor, you have to promote it to others.

WHAT TO DO NEXT?

How entrepreneurial are you? Do you have a mindset oriented toward "what could be?" Here are some next steps to consider.

Putting the Four Entrepreneurship Factors to Work

If you want to grow as an entrepreneurial enterprise leader, devote some of your time each week or month to exploring what you and your organization could do with new products and services. Look at new places and spaces where you could go. Shortly after I arrived at Trevecca in 2013 as their new MBA director, I asked about starting an online MBA program. There was not much support for the idea from the administration or the faculty, because those who work in face-to-face on-campus programs are often reluctant to go online. With the support of the dean of the business school, we were able to launch the MBA program online in 2014. In the first year, online enrollment was only about 15% of the total MBA enrollment. Seven years later in 2021, online enrollment was about 90% of the total MBA enrollment.

As an enterprise leader, you will have to take risks if you are going to pursue new opportunities. I suggest that you avoid the two extremes. The first extreme is to avoid new opportunities because of the risk. The second extreme is to launch into new endeavors without having done your due diligence.

To grow your entrepreneurship, take some time this week or month and list out 3-5 opportunities that you could pursue that would create new value for your stakeholders. The dean of our business school likes to say that all companies are in some way involved in data analytics. With his leadership, we worked on putting together a new data analytics minor track for our MBA students. While getting it up and going did come with several unanticipated speed bumps, with a resourceful team effort, it became an immediate hit its first year. In 2022, we are rolling it out as a stand-alone graduate certificate, with hopes for the program's continued success.

What is it that you could get excited about? How are your promotion skills? Enterprise leaders need to be persuasive in advancing their ideas. What are some next steps you can take to become a more active promoter? One step you could take would be to subscribe to LinkedIn Learning and work through some of their marketing courses. When I logged into my LinkedIn Learning site (yes, I use LinkedIn Learning,), I noticed hundreds of marketing courses with thousands of video segments. Take advantage of their free 30-day trial to watch a short video this week and see if you can advance your enterprise leadership skills in the area of entrepreneurship.

One trap many leaders fall into is focusing on weaknesses. They see where they fall short of the competition and try to innovate around making that weakness stronger. Entrepreneurial leaders do not do this. They innovate in those areas where they are already strong. When you innovate around a weakness, at best you rise to parity with your competition, which is an inefficient use of resources. When you innovate around a strength, you can often generate exponential results and create a sustainable advantage over your competition.

Start Thinking Like an Entrepreneur

Dean refers to this incremental approach to entrepreneurship as the "crawl, walk, run" method. Being the leader of a major organization can often lead to a "go big or go home" mentality, which usually leads to a trip back home. When thinking and acting like an entrepreneur, a part of you has to stop thinking and acting like a big company. You have to think small and be willing to wait for results. This is why most breakthrough innovations come from start-ups and outsiders. The leaders of the big, successful incumbents simply cannot remember how to think small and so they miss the opportunity.

For more on crawl, walk, run, you can read Dean's book by that title which can be found on Amazon.

Using the Canvas for a Startup Idea

The Business Model Canvas, developed by Alexander Osterwalder, has become a very popular method for developing a startup idea. Here are the nine components of the Canvas.

1. **Customer Segments**
   List the top three segments. Look for the segments that provide the most revenue.

2. **Value Proposition**
   What are your products and services? What is the job you get done for your customer?

3. **Revenue Streams**
   List your top three revenue streams. If you do things for free, include them here too.

4. **Channels**
   How do you communicate with your customer? How do you deliver the value proposition?

5. **Customer Relationships**
   How do these show up and how do you maintain the relationship?

6. **Key Activities**
   What do you do every day to run your business model?

7. **Key resources**
   The people, knowledge, means, and money you need to run your business.

8. **Key Partners**
   List the partners (not the suppliers) that you can't do business without.

9. **Cost Structure**
   List your top costs by looking at activities and resources.

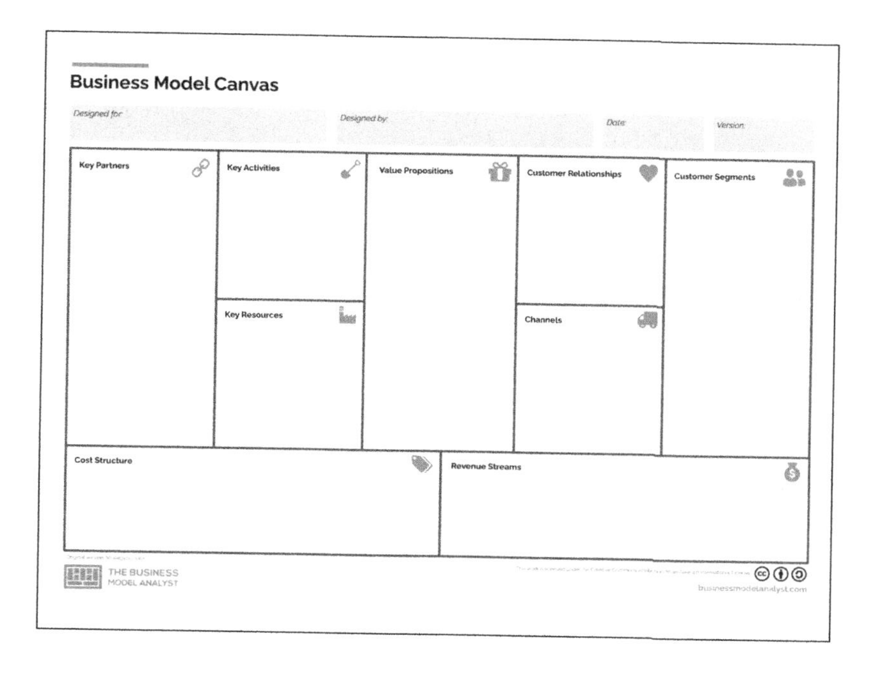

Value Proposition Map

Osterwalder has also developed The Value Proposition Canvas, which includes a Customer Segment Map and Value Proposition Map:

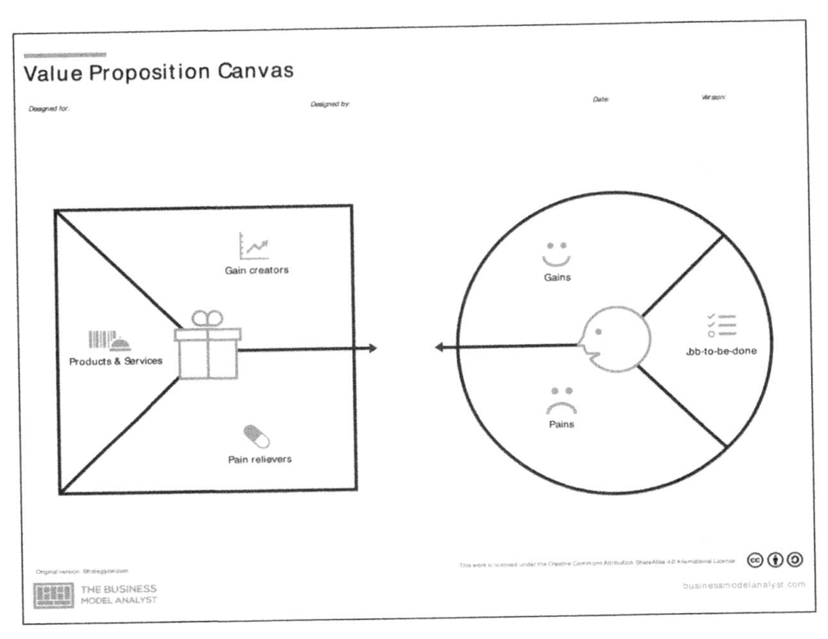

Customer Segment

- Customer Job
- Customer Pain
- Customer Gain

Value Proposition

- Products and Services
- Pain Relievers
- Gain Creators

Start Thinking Like an Entrepreneur

As you seek to grow your entrepreneurial engagement, Schlesinger (2012) and his co-authors have some practical suggestions for how to break out of traditional thinking:

> Our suggestion is to begin thinking like the people who are best at innovating and dealing with the unknown—serial entrepreneurs. After all, there is nothing more uncertain than starting a new business from scratch. In the face of the unknown, serial entrepreneurs act. More specifically they:
>
> 1. Take a small (smart) step forward. In starting a new business, it might be asking potential customers what they think about the idea.
> 2. Pause to see what they learned by doing so. "Gee, the ground seems awfully squishy over there, I better step back and try a different direction." Or, "in talking to people about X they didn't seem all that interested, but they kept telling us over and over again if we tweaked it a bit and..."
> 3. Build that learning into what they do next. It might be presenting a sketch of the modified idea or showing a prototype.

This process is a far cry from the "plan, optimize, execute" of prediction reasoning. But it is precisely the kind of thinking that will let you get out of your own way when you're leading innovation. (para. 8)

Growing as an entrepreneurial enterprise leader doesn't have to be complicated. With focused time and attention, you can move forward in this important area each year.

4.

LEARNING:

Leveraging a Growth Mindset

The new game was to be a 'learn-it-all' company rather than a know-it-all one.

–Sayta Nadella

A growth mindset is different than a fixed mindset. Someone with a fixed mindset sees people as having fixed abilities that don't change much. Maybe you have heard people say, "I'm not good at math," or "I'm not good at languages." A person with fixed mindset believes that you either have it or you don't. Someone with a growth mindset, on the other hand, believes that people can learn almost anything with time and effort.

In an *Inc* (2017) article entitled, "Microsoft's CEO Just Gave Some Brilliant Career Advice. Here it is in 1 Sentence" Satya Nadella says,

> [Carol Dweck's book, *Mindset*] was a huge influence on our family...When I read that book, I realized that the notion of the growth mindset applies to individuals like me and applies to companies like Microsoft. We took that meme of growth mindset and said, let's not be know-it-alls and let's be learn-it-alls. (para. 3)

When I teach a graduate business classes, I can look out at the students and tell who has a fixed mindset. These students' goal is to make sure everyone in the room thinks they are the smartest. The growth mindset students are different. They are curious. They want to learn what they don't yet know.

Some enterprise leaders are know-it-alls, and they are not fun to work with because, like Bill Gates and Steve Balmer at Microsoft, they can be very hard on people. However, growth mindset leaders can also be difficult to work with. They expect everyone to be continuously learning and getting better. Which kind of leader do you want to be?

WHY IT MATTERS

I believe that the world is changing too fast for a fixed mindset. We need a growth mindset across our organizations to keep up with the pace of change. Those who are not continuously learning will lag behind. Ongoing learning is a set of strategies that can keep you current, interested, and relevant. As Geoff Colvin (2008) writes in his book, *Talent is Overrated*:

> You might say that this new understanding [on how to get better] has come along just in the nick of time, because the need for it in every field is greater than ever. The reasons are many. Most apparent is the trend of rapidly rising standards in virtually every domain. To overstate only slightly, people everywhere are doing and making pretty much everything better. (New Findings on Great Performance section)

This learning posture takes discipline. It is easier to have a few early wins in your career and then to ride those wins for years to come. It also takes humility. Learning from others takes a combination of humility, curiosity, hard work, and a natural skepticism of your own bias.

Those who are not continuously learning will lag behind.

HOW IT WORKS

Talent is Overrated

In the introduction to this book, we looked at the insights in Geoff Colvin's book, *Talent is Overrated.* On this topic of talent, we see a truth that has been well-documented by several researchers including:

Carol Dweck, author of *Mindset: The New Psychology of Success* (2006)
Angela Duckworth, author of *Grit: The Power of Passion and Perseverance* (2016)
Ander Erikson, author of *Peak: Secrets from the New Science of Expertise* (2016)

These researchers demonstrate in a variety of ways that when it comes to performance, learning, growth, determination, and development far outpace the role of talent. Becoming an enterprise learner includes moving to a growth mindset.

When it comes to performance, learning, growth, determination, and development far outpace the role of talent.

Growth Mindset vs. Fixed Mindset

The growth mindset framework was largely developed by Carol Dweck (2006). At its core, a growth mindset believes that people can change. This contrasts with a fixed mindset, which insists that people's abilities and weaknesses are stagnant. Microsoft CEO Satya Nadella said that in 2014, Dweck's work on the growth mindset changed his life and leadership and that of Microsoft. In an interview with Jessi Hempel (2019) for LinkedIn, Nadella states:

> If you take two kids at school, one of them has more innate capability but is a know-it-all. The other person has less innate capability but is a learn-it-all. The learn-it-all does better than the know-it-all. (para. 10)

The new game was to be a 'learn-it-all' company rather than a know-it-all one.

A growth mindset puts more focus on effort and progress than on ability. In her key research on "grit," Angela Duckworth (2016) demonstrates that focus and discipline are greater predictors of success than talent. Our goal in coaching leaders is to help our coachees see that they can make progress in almost every area of life through attention and dedication.

As the director of a Chinese Language Program, I worked with a lot of stressed-out adults. Learning Chinese is hard and most days people feel dumb. Fixed mindset students would often lag and just say they weren't good at languages. I would tell them that when I was a grad student, I had a class where we took the Modern Language Aptitude test. Most of my classmates scored in the 90th percentile or higher. I was in the middle at about the 50th percentile. I told these students that learning is not as much about speed as about passion and persistence. For these reasons, I love the title of Angela Duckworth's book, *Grit: The Power of Passion and Perseverance.* For me, I loved the opportunity to talk with people in Chinese. Sure, it might take me twice as long to learn the grammar and vocabulary as compared to some others, but I refused to give up until I could communicate effectively. I reassured our students that they could all learn basic Chinese and learn to communicate with others in daily life. This is a growth mindset.

Even in my sixties, I am still learning by working on my video production skills so that I can improve my instructional videos. Every month, I use LinkedIn Learning to learn something new. This treasure trove of material has thousands of course and tens of thousands of video segments.

Learning from Data

Let's talk about data. Data is everywhere. Some people use data to support their own ideas and biases. I hope we are using data to learn and make better decisions. This past week, I gathered data on our DBA students to see what we could learn about their progress and how we could improve retention. I learned that students without an MBA do about as well as those with an MBA. I also learned which students progressed through the program and which ones tended to struggle.

Even though we live in a world of data analytics, I meet many leaders who want to make decisions based on their own hunches or biases rather than on data. Our goal should be to use data to learn about what is going on around us. Personally, I track my weight, exercise, and time usage. I use this daily data to manage my weight and fitness as well as my use of time.

Today's enterprise leaders are using data both personally and professionally to get better at what they do. Where can you find data and how can you use it to get better at what you do? Remember, data is our friend even when it tells us things that we don't want to know.

I [Dean] like to say to my students and co-workers, if you want to trust your gut, you have to train your gut. How do you train your gut?

Data. If you spend enough time in the data, you can start to rely more on your gut instinct.

There is a trap to data: there is always more. I've known executives who are always looking for that one more piece of data that is going to make it clear what they should do. Data will never remove the need to make choices. For every major decision there comes a point where the data search needs to end and you have to decide. Successful enterprise leaders learn to live with a degree of acceptable ambiguity. They know that data can only inform the decision, not make it for them.

Data Bias

Be on the lookout for data bias. All around us, people are using data to make a certain point, even skewing the data to fit their biases. Consider the difference between the following three statements that each use the same statistic about Americans who like cheese.

- Half of Americans (50%) like cheese.
- The majority of Americans (50%) like cheese.
- Only half of Americans (50%) like cheese.

Sometimes data is used to advance certain brands and boost sales. For example, you might find a food package that will state that the food is gluten free and fat free when all foods of that type are gluten free and fat free. One of my favorite examples of this is licorice. It is not surprising to know that all licorice is gluten free and fat free. It is like saying potato chips are gluten free and dairy free. On a more positive note, we can use food data to make better choices. For example, I learned that I could enjoy a one-scoop raspberry sundae at Culvers for 350 calories instead of a 1,000-calorie two-scoop caramel cashew sundae. Whether it is at home or at work, see if you can put data to work for you and those around you.

Next, reflect on what datasets might provide new insights that could improve your decisions and leadership. Here is a simple example. Look at 20 emails you received in the past hour and decide how many of them are 1) compliance emails that you have to do, 2) aligned with your personal or professional goals, or 3) just a distraction. This might help you to better focus on those emails that matter.

Lastly, you can model this for a team and give them some small assignments related to data and learning. Even a monthly lunch and learn together can help you to build a learning environment.

Iterative Design Cycle / Monthly Strategy Review

In my consulting work, leaders ask me what they should do. I often tell them that we don't know what we don't know. What I mean by this is that sometimes you can only gain insights through experience.

In the previous chapter, I introduced a four-fold framework that promotes iterative learning. Iterative learning happens when you do something and then see what you can learn. This has been going on in science for hundreds of years. Here are the four phases:

1. **Strategic Thinking (Talking):** You begin by thinking of an idea. This can include talking with your team about the idea.
2. **Strategic Planning (Pilot):** Once you have an idea, you put together a plan that will allow you to pilot your idea.
3. **Strategic Acting:** Once your plan and pilot are in place, you put that plan into action.
4. **Strategic Learning:** When your plan and pilot are put into action, you can then learn from what plays out.

This is not a one-time process. As soon as you go through an iteration of these four phases, you can then **re-think** your idea, **re-plan** your next version, and **re-act** by putting it into action. In some cases, you can go through several iterations in just a matter of days.

Let's use the Wright Brothers and the first flight as an example of iterative design. They first thought about what it meant to fly. Like other inventors, they planned a pilot (no pun intended) design for their plane.

They then put that pilot plan into action and evaluated what they had learned. Each iteration helped them learn what they didn't previously know. Once they figured out how to guide a glider in three dimensions (up and down, left and right, as well as rotating), they added power and off they went on the first flight. This took multiple iterations, learning as they went.

In my strategy consulting, I encourage senior teams to iterate to see what they can learn at least every month to see what they can learn. I call this the Monthly Strategy Review. More details on this can be found in the appendix of my book, *Building Strategic Organizations* (2019).

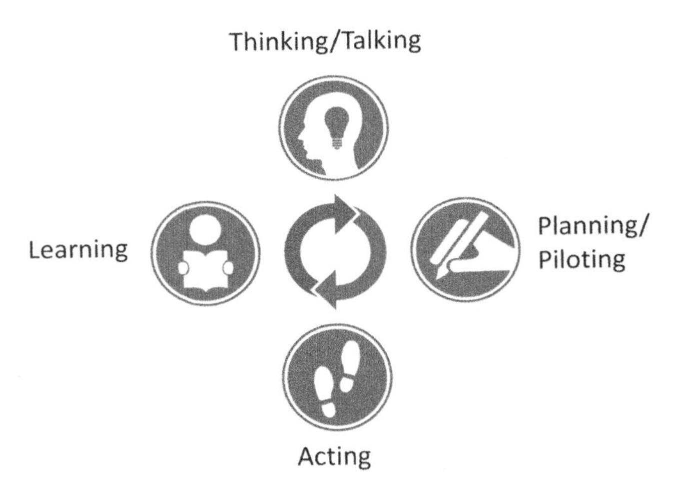

Cross-Discipline Learning

I still remember the day when my son, Jeremy, who was in college at the time told me, "Dad, it is not one thing that sets people apart—it is their ability to combine unlikely combinations that is unique." Today, as mentioned in the previous chapter, Jeremy is Head of School at The Field School in Chicago, an institution that combines 1) a classical approach to education, 2) a Christian focus, and 3) a diverse student body (racially, ethically, and economically). The school has done well over its first five years; some parents have moved across the city and even across the country to enroll their children in a school with this unique blend of features. On this journey, Jeremy has earned a BA degree, two master's degrees, and a PhD in fields as diverse as philosophy, special education, and theology. What combination of features do you and/or your organization bring to your work?

As of 2021, the Taiwan Semiconductor Manufacturing Company (TSMC) has more than half of the global market for made-to-order integrated chips (Campbell, 2021, p. 83). TSMC's iconic founder, Morris Chang, was an active mentor in the life of their current CEO, Mark Liu. Liu emphasizes the need for executives to have a wide variety of experiences:

> That's why I ask our people to get out of their comfort zone to learn things and just feel satisfied getting a good performance review from your boss." (Campbell, 2021, p. 85)

Learning takes time. You don't know what you don't know until you are able to put in the iterations that you need. Hiring people well is a learned skill. When you have hired 100 people over 10 years, you get better at understanding the process, including the critical factors in each stage of hiring.

WHAT TO DO NEXT?

You can begin by taking stock of your current learning pathways. What are you learning? What do you want to be learning? How are you going to move your learning forward? These questions can help you take your learning to the next level.

What Experiments Are You Running?

In the last chapter, we discussed putting experiments to work. Experiments are not just for scientists; they can help leaders and organizations learn about what they don't know. If you don't know much about experiments in the business setting, I recommend starting with the 2011 HBR article, "A Step-by-Step Guide to Smart Business Experiments" by Anderson and Simester.

Your Learning Channels

There are many pathways to learning that you can leverage for your growth and development:

- **Reading:** You may have learned the adage, "leaders are readers." What do you read each month in the way of books and articles?
- **Self-Guided Video Courses:** This is where LinkedIn Learning can be of use.
- **Academic Courses:** Traditional academic courses and online courses can advance your learning.
- **Coaching and Mentoring:** Inviting others into your conversations can accelerate your learning.
- **Learning Communities:** Interacting with others who want to learn can also move you forward.

Each person has a different learning style. See what works for you and keep moving forward. Regardless of the path you choose, life-long learning is a core feature of enterprise leaders.

5.

DISCIPLINE:

Maintaining Focus Over Time

Discipline is choosing between what you want now and what you want most.

–Abraham Lincoln

Most of the readers here are familiar with Jim Collins' iconic 2001 book, *Good to Great,* which remains a best seller to this day. What you probably didn't know is that Collins' book centers around discipline. He writes:

> In a sense, much of this book is about creating **a culture of discipline.** It all starts with **disciplined people**. The transition begins not about trying to discipline the wrong people into the right behaviors, but by getting self-disciplined people on the bus in the first place. Next, we have **disciplined thought**... Finally, we have **disciplined action**. (p. 126)

We will unpack these three disciplines more in the How It Works section below.

WHY IT MATTERS

As we discussed in Chapter 1, focus is one of the central factors that causes leaders and organizations to outperform their peers. Those without focus tend to drift from one thing to another and have a hard time pushing through to sustained excellence. With my coaching and consulting clients, I can see a wide distribution of engagement. Some are very focused on the process and find traction and growth. Others are adrift and often do not gain much from their experience. The same is true for our MBA and DBA students. Grad students without focus are less likely to graduate and less likely to build their toolbox in the process.

HOW IT WORKS

As mentioned above, the goal of enterprise leaders is not to discipline the wrong people. First, enterprise leaders must be disciplined themselves. When I work with MBA and DBA students, some of them struggle to get their work done and eventually drop out. On the one hand, I want all of our students to succeed, but on the other hand, maybe people who struggle with managing their life and work shouldn't have a graduate degree in business. The foundations of enterprise leadership are the habits of focus and discipline. Without these, it is hard to move forward at this level.

Second, the enterprise leader must develop a culture of discipline on their team and within the larger organization. This discipline begins with who you put on the team and then continues as you direct the team toward your preferred outcomes.

Good to Great: Entrepreneurship and Discipline

On the topic of discipline, Collins writes the following in *Good to Great:*

> George Rathmann [CEO of biotech Amgen and Icos] avoided this entrepreneurial death spiral. He understood that the purpose of bureaucracy is to compensate for incompetence and

a lack of discipline—a problem that largely goes away if you have the right people in the first place. (2001, p. 121)

Rathmann also understood an alternative [bureaucracy to manage incompetence and a lack of discipline] exists: Avoid bureaucracy and hierarchy and instead create a culture of discipline. When you put these two complementary forces together—a culture of discipline with an ethic of entrepreneurship—you get a magical alchemy of superior performance and sustained results. (2001, pp. 121-122)

Here is the powerful combination: Entrepreneurship coupled with discipline. In researching this book, I noticed that some people are entrepreneurial, and some are disciplined, but very few are both.

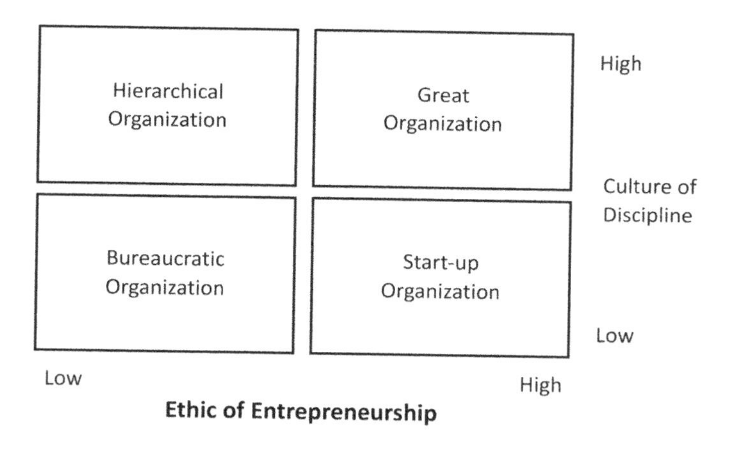

As you can see above, to build a great organization, you need high levels of discipline and high levels of entrepreneurship.

A Culture of Discipline

Collins draws together three concepts in developing a culture of discipline: These include:

- Disciplined People
- Disciplined Thought
- Disciplined Action

In *Good to Great and the Social Sectors* (2005), Collins' follow-up book to *Good to Great,* he emphasizes that the goal of nonprofits is not to become more business-like, but rather to be more disciplined.

> We must reject the idea—well-intentioned, but dead wrong—that the primary path to greatness in the social sectors is to become "more like a business."
>
> Most businesses—like most of anything else in life—fall somewhere between mediocre and good. Few are great.
>
> In my work with nonprofits, I find that they're in desperate need of greater discipline—disciplined planning, disciplined people, disciplined governance, disciplined allocation of resources. (p. 1)

Discipline Can Be Developed

In her book *Grit: The Power of Passion and Perseverance,* Angela Duckworth writes, "One form of perseverance is the daily discipline of trying to do things better than we did yesterday" (2016, Chapter 5). A growth mindset with perseverance can result in greater discipline moving forward. Let's look at some next steps in this important area.

WHAT TO DO NEXT?

"Rick, I don't remember you as being a good student or overly religious," one of my classmates remarked at an induction ceremony for outstanding alumni from my high school. In high school, I was more about sports and trouble than academics or church. When I became a Christian in college, things began to change. My journey of spiritual and academic growth along with patient input from my wife, Cheri, helped develop my focus and discipline.

Developing Willpower

The good news is that, like your physical muscles, discipline can also be developed. Heidi Halvorson Grant addresses this in her book, *Nine Things that Successful People Do Differently* (2012). Here she writes on the relationship between discipline, self-control, and willpower:

> Your self-control "muscle" is just like the other muscles in your body; when it doesn't get much exercise, it becomes weaker over time. But when you give it regular workouts by putting it to good use, it will grow stronger and stronger, and better able to help you successfully reach your goals. To build willpower, take on a challenge that requires you to do something you'd honestly rather not do. Give up high-fat snacks, do a hundred sit-ups a day, stand up straight when you catch yourself slouching, try to learn a new skill. When you find yourself wanting to give in, give up, or just not bother—don't.
>
> Start with just one activity and make a plan for how you will deal with troubles when they occur ("If I have a craving for a snack, I will eat one piece of fresh or three pieces of dried fruit"). It will be hard in the beginning, but it will get easier, and that's the whole point. As your strength grows, you can take on more challenges and step up your self-control workout. (Build Your Willpower Muscle section)

[Dean] The other good news is that, unlike your physical muscles, developing willpower in one area of your life strengthens your ability to apply more willpower to other areas of your life. Charles Duhigg, describes this phenomenon in his book *The Power of Habit*:

> As people strengthened their willpower muscles in one part of their lives—in the gym, or a money management program—that strength spilled over into what they ate or how hard they worked. Once willpower became stronger, it touched everything. (2012, p. 139)

How Did I Earn a Doctoral Degree?

I still remember how, on the first day of my doctoral program, the dean said, "Look to your left. Look to your right. Only one of you will graduate." He was emphasizing that the graduation rate was less than 50%. That day, I felt like I was one of the dumbest students in the group because I didn't have a masters in the field like most of the other students did. I pressed on. I didn't quit. I graduated and it changed the entire trajectory of my future life and work.

Over time, I have developed the Two Mann Commandments for my grad students. They consist of just 10 words: "Never hand in late work and get better each week." Focus and discipline are all it takes to succeed at these injunctions. I did it and most of my students can do it as well.

Take a few minutes to complete the FIELD tools assessment found in the appendix of this book. They will help you to better understand where you are at now and where you need to develop.

Practice, Practice, Practice

At the end of 2021, I met with my coach, as I do each month. Together, we went over my goals for 2022. These typically include:

- The goal or objective (what you call it doesn't matter)
- The data to be collected each month
- The desired thresholds
- A monthly check-in time

Let me give you a couple of examples:

- Maintain a healthy weight
- Collect daily weigh-in data
- Average 169-170 lbs for the year
- Review with my coach each month

Here is a second example:

- Exert my body through exercise each week
- Collect daily max heartrate data each day
- Exceed 150 bpm each day for at least 5 days a week
- Review with coach each month

Toward the end of our coaching session, I asked my coach if he has many clients who do this. He said, "Many people set goals, but not many identify the data and track it to see if they are meeting their goal thresholds." I find the same thing is true with many people I coach.

If you want to grow personally and professionally, it can help to set some goals (establish focus) and track them over time (discipline). As you assess your own level of focus, you can begin by looking at your tendencies. Do you start well and finish well? Leaders with greater focus begin with the end in mind. They are outcomes oriented. They have grit as defined in the title of Angela Duckworth's book, *Grit: The Power of Passion and Perseverance.* Passion helps us to focus, while perseverance helps us to maintain that focus over time.

CONCLUSION

In this book, we have covered these five FIELD Tools:

- Focus
- Innovation
- Entrepreneurship
- Learning
- Discipline

Getting traction on all five of these is not an easy task. That is why enterprise leaders are not common. As Jim Collins puts it in *Good to Great,* high levels of entrepreneurship and discipline are what powers great enterprise leaders and great organizations.

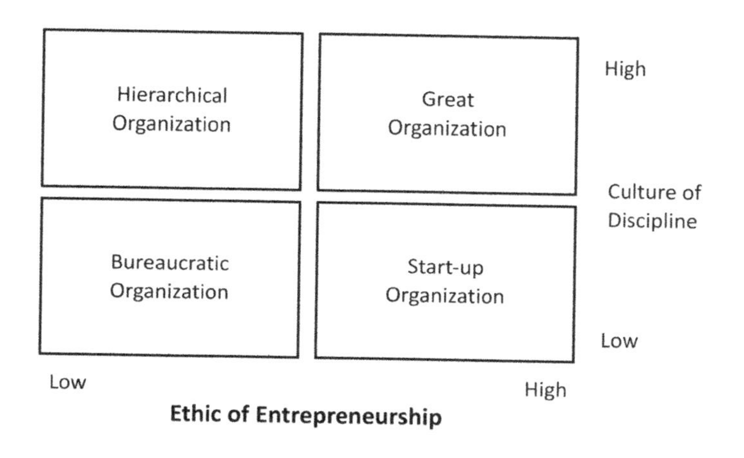

I do hope that you will press on in your enterprise leadership journey and in developing enterprise leaders within your organization. The need for enterprise leaders is so great, and the supply is so low, that we need to do all we can to grow the enterprise leaders in our organizations. If we succeed, we can build a better world. If we can be of help on your enterprise leadership journey, please feel free to contact Rick at 615-268-0596 or Rick@ClarionStrategy.com.

APPENDIX A:

FIELD TOOLS ASSESSMENT

You can use this assessment with you and your team to see where your strengths and weaknesses might be.

Focus: Developing Bifocal Vision
Focus is about your ability to stay with something without getting distracted or losing interest.

5. Great
4. Good
3. Adequate
2. Poor
1. Train Wreck or Missing

Innovation: Moving Toward Greater Value
Innovation is about your active engagement and ability to improve the value that you and your team create for others.

5. Great
4. Good
3. Adequate
2. Poor
1. Train Wreck or Missing

Entrepreneurship: Pursuing New Opportunities

Entrepreneurship is about your desire and willingness to develop new opportunities around you.

5. Great
4. Good
3. Adequate
2. Poor
1. Train Wreck or Missing

Learning: Leveraging a Growth Mindset

Learning is about reflecting and engaging on your experience and data sets in ways that lead to continued growth and development.

5. Great
4. Good
3. Adequate
2. Poor
1. Train Wreck or Missing

Discipline: Maintaining Focus Over Time

Discipline is staying with something with perseverance so that you regularly move to completion and achieve your goals.

5. Great
4. Good
3. Adequate
2. Poor
1. Train Wreck or Missing

Overall Total: ________

Great: 22-25, Good: 18-21, Adequate: 14-17,
Poor: 10-13, Train Wreck: <10

APPENDIX B:

GRIT SCALE

The following was developed by Angela Duckworth. The Grit Scale is listed at the end.

1. New ideas and projects sometimes distract me from previous ones.

1. Very much like me
2. Mostly like me
3. Somewhat like me
4. Not much like me
5. Not like me at all

2. Setbacks don't discourage me. I don't give up easily.

5. Very much like me
4. Mostly like me
3. Somewhat like me
2. Not much like me
1. Not like me at all

3. I often set a goal but later choose to pursue a different one.

1. Very much like me
2. Mostly like me

3. Somewhat like me
4. Not much like me
5. Not like me at all

4. I am a hard worker.

5. Very much like me
4. Mostly like me
3. Somewhat like me
2. Not much like me
1. Not like me at all

5. I have difficulty maintaining my focus on projects that take more than a few months to complete.

1. Very much like me
2. Mostly like me
3. Somewhat like me
4. Not much like me
5. Not like me at all

6. I finish whatever I begin.

5. Very much like me
4. Mostly like me
3. Somewhat like me
2. Not much like me
1. Not like me at all

7. My interests change from year to year.

1. Very much like me
2. Mostly like me
3. Somewhat like me
4. Not much like me
5. Not like me at all

8. I am diligent. I never give up.

5. Very much like me
4. Mostly like me
3. Somewhat like me
2. Not much like me
1. Not like me at all

9. I have been obsessed with a certain idea or project for a short time but later lost interest.

1. Very much like me
2. Mostly like me
3. Somewhat like me
4. Not much like me
5. Not like me at all

10. I have overcome setbacks to conquer an important challenge.

5. Very much like me
4. Mostly like me
3. Somewhat like me
2. Not much like me
1. Not like me at all

Scoring:

1. For questions 1, 4, 6, 9, 10 and 12 assign the following points:

   5 = Very much like me

   4 = Mostly like me

   3 = Somewhat like me

   2 = Not much like me

   1 = Not like me at all

2. For questions 2, 3, 5, 7, 8 and 11 assign the following points:
   1 = Very much like me
   2 = Mostly like me
   3 = Somewhat like me
   4 = Not much like me
   5 = Not like me at all

Add up all the points and divide by 12.

The maximum score on this scale is 5 (extremely gritty), and the lowest scale on this scale is 1 (not at all gritty).

Distribution:

10%	2.5
20%	3.0
30%	3.3
40%	3.5
50%	3.8
60%	3.9
70%	4.1
80%	4.3
90%	4.5
95%	4.7
99%	4.9

APPENDIX C:

RECOMMENDED READING

Articles

The Innovator's DNA – Dyer, Gregersen, and Christensen

ClarionToolBox Series

- *Strategic Leaders are Made, Not Born*
- *Building Strategic Organizations*
- *Strategic Finance for Strategic Leaders*
- *Coaching: The First Five Tools for Strategic Leaders*
- Under development
    - *Nonprofit Leadership and Management*
    - *The Leadership Journey*
    - *The First Five Tools for SUCCESS in College, Graduate School, Life, and Work*

Harvard Business Review (HBR) Leadership and Strategy Boxed Set

- *Blue Ocean Strategy* – Kim and Mauborgne
- *The Innovator's Dilemma* – Clay Christensen
- *Leading Change* – John Kotter
- *Playing to Win* – Lafley and Martin
- *Financial Intelligence* – Berman and Knight

Other Books

- *Good to Great* – Collins
- *Good to Great and the Social Sector* – Collins
- *Scaling Up: How a Few Companies...And Why the Rest Don't* – Harnish
- *How Will You Measure Your Life?* – Christensen

Harvard Business Review

Over 30 years ago, I asked an internationally-known nonprofit leader what I should read. He said, "Read *Harvard Business Review*." I scoffed at his answer, saying to myself that I wanted to change the world and didn't have the time or the interest to read HBR. In recent years, I went back to that leader and told him how dumb I was. Today, I read every HBR issue cover to cover. The topics covered are much broader than just business. Therefore, when people ask me what they should do if they don't have the time or the money for an MBA, I recommend HBR. To graduating MBA students who ask what they should do next, I say read HBR. That includes about everyone who wants to grow as a strategic leader.

For about $100 a year, you can get both the paper copy and digital access to current and past articles. HBR offers a treasure chest of insight on many business and non-business topics.

APPENDIX D:

GETTING BIGGER AND BETTER

When I am coaching organizational leaders, I will ask them, "Where do you want to go and how can I help?" The most common answer I get is that they want their organization to get bigger and better and they usually say it in that order. I will address these under the headings of Scaling and Improving, but in a different order. In my experience, getting better is a good first step toward getting bigger.

Enterprise leaders are often tasked to lead these ambitious goals of getting bigger and better. Let's look at each of these and some of the issues involved.

IMPROVING

"Rick, the key to marketing is having something good to sell," the marketing director at the organization where I worked told me. Yes, if you want to get bigger, the first place to start is by getting better.

Many organizations struggle because they do not put adequate evaluation systems in place. This makes improving elusive. I suggest organizations work through some basic strategic planning processes. Here is a simple, five-fold process you can work through.

MV3: Begin by affirming your:

- Mission
- Vision
- Values
- Value Proposition(s)

In my experience, it is most common to lack clarity around the main value propositions.

- **Strategic Themes:** These are your 1-3 big deals or priorities for this year and next.
- **Strategic Objectives:** These objectives are a balanced set of strategies for each theme.
- **Strategic Measures:** Choose 3-5 for each strategic theme. Try to include some measures that are tracked monthly and quarterly rather than having the bulk of your measure tracked annually.
- **Strategic Initiatives:** In a page or so, outline key projects that represent an allocation of TEMP (Time, Energy, Money, and People) resources that will advance your key measures.

You can put these strategic planning basics together in just a few pages. Working through this and being "on the same page" can be invaluable for your team.

One you get into a monthly strategy review (MSR), you are in a better place to move toward continuous improvement.

You also may want to ask your end-users for their feedback each quarter or year.

NOTE: The ClarionToolBox book, *Building Strategic Organizations: The First Five Tools for Strategy and Strategic*

Planning goes into more detail on this five-fold strategic planning process.

SCALING

"What would you like to do going forward?" I asked. "We would like to double in size over the next decade." These "double in a decade" plans can work if they are adequately planned and executed. When due diligence is not done on the front end, execution often struggles.

Planning for Growth

Significant growth or scaling up requires ongoing intentionality. You and your organization will need to do some new things to support this level of new growth.

- **Clarifying the Path Forward**: First, on one piece of paper, write down **where** you hope to be by **when**. If you want to "double in a decade," that could be doubling revenue, headcount, sales, locations, etc. Try to clarify what you can in a draft and then pass the page around to get input and buy-in from your key stakeholders.
- **Outlining Needed Resources:** Once you have a roadmap, look at what TEMP resources you will need at each point along the way. For example, when we started the nursing program at Crown College, we needed to have the Director of Nursing in place a year before we had our first students. I like using a 4x5 forecasting tool for this. This simple process looks at the following areas over five fiscal years:
    - **Assumptions (Volume/Rates)**: numbers of people, customers, end-users, financial pricing, rates, etc.
    - **Revenue**: What (if any) revenue do you expect?
    - **Expenses**: What expenses do you anticipate?
    - **Net Income**: Revenue minus Expenses.

Here is a sample 4x5 taken from the ClarionToolBox book, *Strategic Finance for Strategic Leaders* (2020).

New Project (4x5)		FY1	FY2	FY3	FY4	FY5
Volume/Rates						
	Students per week	28.00				
	Student Rate per hour	$ 35.00				
	Tutor pay per hour	$ 17.50				
	Hours per week	2.00				
	Weeks per year	50.00				
Revenue						
	Tutoring Fees	$ 98,000.00				
	Revenue Total	**$ 98,000.00**				
Expense						
	Tutor pay	$ 49,000.00				
	Rent	$ 12,000.00				
	Depreciation	$ 5,000.00				
	Total Expense	**$ 66,000.00**				
Income from Operations						
	Earnings before Interest/Taxes (EBIT)	**$ 32,000.00**				
Other Expenses						
	Interest	$ 5,000.00				
Income before Taxes		**$ 27,000.00**				
	Income Taxes (30%)	$ 8,100.00				
Net Income						
	Net Income from Operations	$ 18,900.00				
Changes in Cash Flows						
	Income from Operations	$ 18,900.00				
	+ Depreciation	$ 5,000.00				
	- Capital Expenditures	$ (25,000.00)				
	- Principle Paid	$ (5,000.00)				
	Change in Cash	$ (6,100.00)				

- **Moving Forward**: One you have an agreed-upon plan and the necessary resources in place, you are ready to move forward. Hopefully, you can review the strategic measures on your 4x5 each month or quarter to see if you are on track with your growth and expansion. As your projects unfold each quarter, you can see whether your investment of TEMP resources is providing you with the ROI that you intended. If things are lagging, you may need to reallocate your projects and resources to better accomplish your desired outcomes.
- **Inputs and Outcomes:** Significant growth and scaling will require a combination of strategic inputs as well as the continued monitoring of your outcomes. The key problem to avoid here is confusing inputs and outcomes. Many leaders and organizations will say that things are going well because people are working hard. It is easier than you might think to have everyone working hard while the outcome of "doubling in a decade" languishes. If outcomes are lagging, you may need to revisit your allocation of resources and/or revisit your outcome goals.

APPENDIX E:

THE FIVE FOUNDATIONAL RS OF SUCCESS

I have had the privilege of working with hundreds and hundreds of college students, graduate students, and employees for over 30 years. As a natural people watcher as well as a trained social-science researcher, I have seen some patterns of success. On this journey, I have also benefited from reading some of the best research on human development, adult learning, and effectiveness in the workplace.

Through this journey, I have put together this material on the Five Rs. Over two decades ago, through parenting and leading, I settled on the first three Rs, which include being relational, responsible, and resourceful. In many ways, these three are not only supported by the research but also by common sense. The fourth and fifth tools, resilience and realistic have been added in light of the abundance of research on these topics over the last decade. The Five Rs include:

- Relational
- Responsible
- Resourceful
- Resilient
- Realistic

INTRODUCTION

Overall, these Five Rs are not age dependent. In many cases, these are largely functional in the lives of many teens. Generally, these characteristics should be improving as teens and young adults move from 13 to 30 years old. The earlier these 5 Rs are working well, the more value a person can bring to their stakeholders in life and work.

I did not learn these five tools until I was older (read: out of college). I am thankful for my wife, Cheri, some good counselors, and God's work in my life as an adult between 20 and 40 years old. It is never too late to experience growth in these five areas. Based on Carol Dweck's research on the Growth Mindset, we now know that these 5Rs can be strengthened at any age. Let's unpack each of these five tools.

RELATIONAL:

"HEALTHY GIVE-AND-TAKE IN RELATIONSHIPS"

Relationships are central to life, work, and leadership. Have you ever lived and worked with high-maintenance people? It is not fun. These are not the people that you want on your team. Sometimes you don't have a choice. You, however, do not want to be this person. Relational people have a higher EQ, are more empathetic, and are able to balance the care they provide for others and the care they receive.

Obviously, you do not want to be someone who only cares about themselves. Nor do you want to wear yourself out by only serving those around you. The key is the right balance of give and take.

> **Next Steps**: Where are you in this balancing act? Do you serve others well? Do you have relationships that are life-giving? Assess where you are at and what some appropriate next steps might be. At times, I have found that a capable counselor with the right chemistry was able to help me sort this out. In addition,

you might want to move away from draining relationships and toward life-giving relationships.

RESPONSIBLE:
"CONSISTENTLY MEETING AGREED-UPON COMMITMENTS"

We all want to work with people who do what they say they are going to do. You do not want people on your team who consistently over-promise and under-deliver. The first Mann Commandment I give to my grad students is made up of these five words: "Never hand in late work." Why do I emphasize this? Handing in late work is the #1 reason why students fail out of our MBA program. This doesn't mean you have to say yes to everyone and everything. It just means that you need to follow through on what you commit to.

Responsible people do not blame others when they come up short. One thing I notice with our under-achieving MBA students is their tendency to blame others when things don't go well.

Next Steps: Do you over-promise and under-deliver? How are you doing at meeting agreed-upon deadlines? Ask people around you what they think about your follow-through.

RESOURCEFUL:
"ACCOMPLISHING YOUR GOALS WITH LIMITED RESOURCES"

Every day, most of us are faced with the challenges of limited TEMP resources. TEMP resources are Time, Energy, Money, and People. Meeting your goals with limited resources requires resourcefulness. If I am a team leader, I look for people who are resourceful. These are people who can figure out how to get the job done with fewer TEMP resources than we would all like.

Next Steps: A good place to start on resourcefulness is planning ahead. When you look forward at what you have to do and reflect on what you have, you are better able to think through the best use of your limited TEMP resources. Look back and see where you could have achieved your goals even with limited resources.

RESILIENT:

"POSITIVELY MOVING THROUGH DIFFICULTIES"

In life and work, difficulties will come. The question is whether we can press through when we get knocked down or things don't go our way. Moving forward with an attitude of hope is a capacity that is crucial, but not common. You don't have to do this on your own. Sometimes the healthy thing to do is to involve others as you journey through difficulties.

Next Steps: When you look back, how have you done on working through difficulties? Do you have some unprocessed issues that need to be addressed?

REALISTIC:

"HAVING HOPE BUT KNOWING THAT THE ROAD TO SUCCESS WILL BE CHALLENGING"

Decades ago, Albert Bandura, a pioneer in psychology, put forth the durable hypothesis that one of the best predictors is believing that you will succeed. Being an optimist is better than being a pessimist. Being a realistic optimist is the best of all. Heidi Grant, the author of the book *Succeed*, writes, "Believing that the road to success will be rocky leads to greater success because it forces you to take action" (p. 19).

Next Steps: Are you naturally pessimistic or optimistic? Realistic optimism can be learned and put into practice every day. See what you can do to move forward in a way that is both optimistic and realistic.

Going Forward

To summarize these five Rs, we have:

- Relational
- Responsible
- Resourceful
- Resilient
- Realistic

Only you can assess where you are at in these five areas. A place to start is to ask:

- Which of these five Rs is your strongest area?
- Which of these areas need the most growth?

All of us have room for growth somewhere. Think through these and talk with those close to you to identify what your growth areas might be. You can do this with family members, friends, and co-workers.

Lastly, the goal here is not to grit your teeth and press forward. Instead, this is like training for a marathon. Even small steps can move you forward. These steps have the potential to set you up for a different future. Choose an area today and think through some practical steps to move forward.

If I can be of help on these topics, please feel free to email me at Rick@ClarionStrategy.com.

APPENDIX F:

THE LEADERSHIP JOURNEY

I have learned a lot by working with over 1,000 grad students who have sought to gain a credible graduate-degree credential. What I have realized as I have worked with and developed leaders is that there is more to leadership development than just getting an academic credential. I will sometimes say, "An MBA does not automatically make a manager or leader, but it can help." Similarly, a seminary degree does not automatically produce a capable pastor, but it can help."

OVERVIEW

As we look at the leadership development process, we can consider these several layers or stages:

1. Character
2. Work Ethic
3. Toolbox
4. Experience
5. Credentials

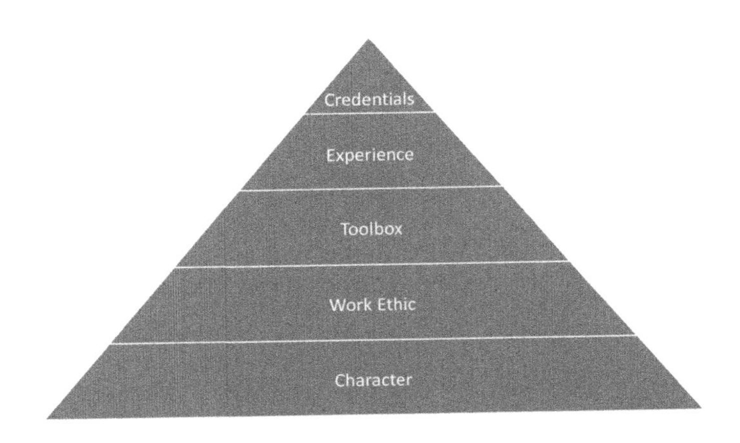

When I work with graduate students, they are looking at adding a credential to their portfolio. I like to emphasize to them, that a credential with character and work ethic doesn't help anyone. Instead, I think the journey looks something like this.

A person with great character and a strong work ethic will most likely be successful in this world. Add tactical, strategic, and visionary tools to their toolbox and they can be a great team leader. Give this person the right experiences along the way and they can develop even further and go even farther in their leadership journey. Lastly, a credential like an MBA can open doors of opportunity where they can put their character, work ethic, tools, and experiences to greater use.

I am saddened when I see students with graduate degrees who are missing the four layers below credentials. Ideally, students build these layers along the way to ensure a strong future.

CHARACTER

I have often asked, "how many smart, dishonest accountants do we need?" The answer is none. The starting point of compelling leadership is character. We have all seen leaders with and without solid character.

Let's look at these areas of leadership.

- **Honesty and Integrity**: The basics of character are honesty and integrity. This is doing the right thing when no one is looking.
- **Care and Empathy for others**: Leaders with strong character care about others and are able to empathize with those facing difficulties.
- **Self-Awareness:** Knowing thyself is foundational to strong character.
- **Humility and Teachability**: Leaders with strong character do not have to be the smartest person in the room. They are able to humbly learn from others.
- **Servant Leadership**: Most good leaders know that leadership is not about them, it is about collaborating with others. Servant leaders seek to support, build, and develop those around them.

When Missing: When character is missing, leaders tend to go toxic. If you or others can't or don't develop a foundation of good character, it is time to start over. Lastly, I like to say, "Not all leaders are mature, and not all mature leaders are mature all the time." This means there is a difference between those with fundamentally flawed character and those who have sound character but at times show lapses in good judgement.

WORK ETHIC

With foundational character in place, we can now look at work ethic. A strong work ethic includes:

- **Time:** Part of working hard is just putting in the needed time. This doesn't have to mean 100-hr weeks, but it does mean focused hours.

- **Effort**: Sometimes effort is more important than time. Effort is leaning into what is in front of you, so that your time is maximized.
- **Curiosity**: As you put in the time and effort, we want to see curiosity as well. Curiosity allows you to learn as you work. What are you learning from what you are doing? Even boring activities can provide learning opportunities.
- **Professional Practice**: We sometimes think of work ethic in blue collar terms. A strong work ethic for strategic leaders relates to professional practice. Professional practice includes areas like being on time, meeting agreed-upon deadlines, and attention to detail.
- I have met great leaders who don't work long hours. They are very good at taking the hours they have and leaning into them with strong focus, effect, curiosity, and intentionality.

When Missing: When a strong work ethic is missing, leadership development is slowed and long-term leadership potential is limited.

TOOLBOX

When students study for an MBA or other degree, they have the opportunity to learn and to put a number of tools in their toolbox. This can include becoming a better writer, sharpening analysis skills, or becoming better at making presentations. These tools help them to build a stronger leadership future. We can break tools into three categories:

- **Tactical**: These are the practical tools like time and task management.
- **Strategic**: Tools at this level could include SWOT analysis; understanding net present value; and using measures to make better decisions.

- **Visionary**: These tools help you to be inspirational, aligning people toward a common goal.

Related to these different categories of skills and tools is an understanding that development is needed on the technical side of leadership as well as on the soft side. The soft side includes the emotional and relational, as well as the ability to align and inspire people on the team.

When Missing: A leader with good character and a strong work ethic can do a lot. Think of them like carpenters who put in the work to build a garage. However, put the right tools in their hands and those carpenters can build that garage better and faster.

EXPERIENCE

If we take a younger professional with good character, a strong work ethic, and a deep toolbox, they are at a great place. Imagine the next 10 years. They have a lot to contribute as a team member. If they get an opportunity to be an assistant team leader at 3 years and a team leader at 6 years, they will be in a much stronger place at year 10. The key to getting the right experience is getting opportunities that are stretching but not overwhelming. Getting the right new experiences at the right times is invaluable in accelerating a person's leadership development.

When Missing: When these experience opportunities are missing, nothing bad happens, but growth is stunted. What could have been developed is missed.

CREDENTIALS

I earned my doctoral degree just before I turned 30. Over the following decades, that credential opened many doors for new leadership opportunities. When a person has the right credentials with the previous four layers, it is a powerful combination.

When Missing: A credential is a signal to others that you have a deep toolbox. When you don't have that credential, it is harder to send those signals.

GOING FORWARD

Take some time to do an inventory as to where you are and what needs to be developed going forward. Involve those around you who can help you on this journey, including:

- Family members: Parents, spouse, children, and others.
- Friends who know you well, are supportive, and will be honest with you.
- Co-workers: Supervisors, peers, subordinates.
- Professors: Faculty members.
- Coaches and mentors.

DOES THE ORDER MATTER?

In some ways, yes, and it some ways, no. I believe that character needs to come first because it is the most foundational. You can develop your toolbox before and after your experience, but I suggest that students view their academic work as a way to build their toolbox. While I believe that getting experience before a grad degree is ideal, that is often not the case. Doing three grad degrees before I turned 30 opened some doors to further experiences. Obviously, we want physicians to get their degrees before they get their experience. So, does the order of these five phases matter? Yes and no.

ABOUT THE AUTHORS:

Two Case Studies

The two authors of this book have embarked on their own enterprise leadership journeys with some similarities and many differences. Rick and Dean both started off as public-school teachers and then moved on. They were both later MBA students later in life. The following section provides more details about their journeys.

Rick Mann, PhD

I was not a good student growing up. I didn't really like school. I got into lots of trouble as a teen, but I did enjoy wrestling when I was in high school, an activity that would prove helpful later in life. The summer after high school graduation forever changed my life. A friend of mine from high school invited me to church. I wasn't interested in church, but I was interested in her, so I agreed to go. Here, I heard for the first time about the opportunity for new life in Christ. That day, I committed my life to Christ and things have not been the same since.

In the middle of college, Cheri and I got married. Not a plan I would recommend. However, after 40-plus years of marriage, I have to say that she has been instrumental to my growth and development. After college, we heard about the opportunity for teachers in China. This led me to complete an MDiv in Chinese Studies as well as an MA and PhD at Ohio State. In the 80s, off we went to China and early on my leadership grew through the opportunity to supervise teachers across China. Part of the leadership journey is getting early experience leading a team. In China, I had two entrepreneurial opportunities to start: 1) An academic journal, and 2) a Chinese language program. In the Chinese language program, I also had the opportunity to pioneer some innovative strategies. With some of Cheri's continued health issues, we eventually relocated to the States. Here I had the opportunity to be the lead pastor of a growing church. It was during these years that I began to coach others and to develop coaching networks. The next leadership opportunity came when I served as the VP/Academic Affairs and then Provost at Crown College in Minnesota. When the previous president left, I then served as the president for eight years. When Cheri had some health issues that required that us to move to a warmer climate, I had the opportunity to lead the MBA program and then start the DBA program at Trevecca Nazarene University.

For that last 10-plus years, I have also had the opportunity to serve as the Managing Director of ClarionStrategy, a coaching and consulting firm. This gave me the opportunity to work with senior leaders in organizations both small and large with annual revenues that ranged from $100,000 to over $500 million.

Today, I look back on my own enterprise leadership journey and the privilege I continue to have in helping leaders and organizations on their own enterprise leadership journeys.

Dean Diehl, EdD

From the age of 15, I knew I wanted to be a teacher. I was a young man on a mission, serving and equipping myself throughout high school and college with a passion and commitment to be well-prepared to teach. I landed my first job as a high school band director at the age of 23. I quit just three years later frustrated, empty, and burnt out. This was my first identity crisis.

While I was struggling to find myself after walking away from a decade-long dream, I ended up in the sales department of a small, independently owned music company. The company was so small it did not have a marketing department and so I found myself volunteering to take on more and more of the advertising and merchandising responsibilities until I was eventually made the director of marketing and given a small team to lead.

Over the next ten years, that company grew from $3 million to over $30 million in annual sales and was purchased by Zomba Music Group, one of the largest independent music companies in the world. Eventually, our division became part of Sony Music, Inc. and I was elevated to Senior Vice President of Marketing, with responsibility for three record labels, a film division, and a music publishing company.

My second identity crisis came about when I turned 46. It was during the Christmas holidays, a time I always use to do some vision casting and dreaming about the future. I realized that, while I was very successful in a job I was good at and liked, deep inside I was not happy.

You see, I had never set out to have a career in the music business. It just happened. One thing led to another, I got busy, and twenty years went by in a flash. It was time to start being intentional and to take hold of my life and choose a direction instead of being swept along. I chose to go back to my first dream, teaching.

So, I quit my high-paying executive job to teach Music Business at a small Christian university in the heart of Nashville, Tennessee. I took an 80% pay cut, took on a couple of consulting gigs to make ends meet, and started the journey of a lifetime. Along the way I picked up an

MBA in Marketing and an Ed.D. in Leadership. I also returned to Sony as a part-time executive with responsibility for shaping enterprise-level strategy for their collection of faith-based divisions collectively referred to as Provident Entertainment.

Throughout my career, I have developed some core philosophies about leading at the enterprise level, which I will briefly share here.

- Work Hard
- Think Deep
- Constantly Scan the Horizon
- Be Kind
- Find the Win/Win
- Be Flexible and Adapt
- Invest in People
- Innovate…Then Innovate Some More!
- Have Faith in Something Bigger Than Yourself

Finally, We Spend Most of Our Lives Working…Find Work Worth the Sacrifice.

REFERENCES

Blank, S. (2013). Why the lean start-Up changes everything. *Harvard Business Review*. https://hbr.org/2013/05/why-the-lean-start-up-changes-everything

Christensen, C. (1997). *The innovator's dilemma: When new technologies cause great firms to fail* (Reprint ed.). Harvard Business Review Press.

Christensen, C. M., Raynor, M. E., & McDonald, R. (2015). What Is disruptive innovation? *Harvard Business Review*. https://hbr.org/2015/12/what-is-disruptive-innovation

Creating enterprise leaders. (2015). CEB HR Leadership Council.

Diehl, D. (2019). *Was on-demand music streaming a disruptive innovation?*

Drucker, P. F. (2002a). The discipline of innovation. *Harvard Business Review*. https://hbr.org/2002/08/the-discipline-of-innovation

Drucker, P. F. (2002b). The discipline of innovation. *Harvard Business Review*. https://hbr.org/2002/08/the-discipline-of-innovation

Duckworth, A. (2016). *Grit: The power of passion and perserverence*. Scribner.

Duhigg, C. (2016). *Smarter, faster, better: The secrets of being productive in life and business*. Random House.

Dweck, C. (2006). *Mindset: The new psychology of success*. Ballantine Books.

Dweck, C. (2016). What having a "growth mindset" actually means. *Harvard Business Review*. https://hbr.org/2016/01/what-having-a-growth-mindset-actually-means

Dyer, J. H., Gregersen, H., & Christensen, C. M. (2009). The innovator's DNA. *Harvard Business Review*. https://hbr.org/2009/12/the-innovators-dna

Eisenmann, T. (2013). Entrepreneurship: A working definition. *Harvard Business Review*. https://hbr.org/2013/01/what-is-entrepreneurship

Enterprise leadership: Developing new leadership for a new world. (2021). Korn Ferry.

Fossett, J., Gilchrist, D., & Luca, M. (2018). Using experiments to launch new products. *Harvard Business Review*. https://hbr.org/2018/11/using-experiments-to-launch-new-products

Halvorson, H. (2010). *Succeed: How we can reach our goals*. Plume.

Halvorson, H. (2011). *Nine things successful people do differently*. Harvard Business Review Press.

Kets de Vries, M. (2014). Coaching the toxic leader. *Harvard Business Review*. https://hbr.org/2014/04/coaching-the-toxic-leader

Kirsner, S. (2018). The biggest obstacles to innovation at large companies. *Harvard Business Review*. https://hbr.org/2018/07/the-biggest-obstacles-to-innovation-in-large-companies

Kislik, L. (2017). What to do if your boss gets distracted by every new thing. *Harvard Business Review*. https://hbr.org/2017/11/what-to-do-if-your-boss-gets-distracted-by-every-new-thing

Kotter, J. (1990). *Force for change: How leadership differs from management*. Free Press.

Kotter, J. (2012). *Leading change*. Harvard Business Review Press.

Mann, R. (2019a). *Building strategic organizations: The first five tools for strategy and strategic planning*. ClarionStrategy.

Mann, R. (2019b). *Strategic leaders are made, not born: The first five tools for escaping the tactical tsunami*. ClarionStrategy.

Morin, A. (2014). *13 things mentally strong people don't do: Take back your power, embrace change, face your fears, and train your brain for happiness and success.* William Morrow.

Ready, D. A., & Peebles, M. E. (2015). *Developing the next generation of enterprise leaders.* MIT Sloan Management Review. https://sloanreview.mit.edu/article/developing-the-next-generation-of-enterprise-leaders/

Ries, E. (2011). *The lean startup: How today's entrepreneurs use continuous innovation to create radically successful businesses.* Crown.

Rumelt, R. P. (2011). *Good strategy, bad strategy: The difference and why it matters.* Crown Business.

Schlesinger, L., Kiefer, C., & Brown, P. (2012). *The biggest obstacle to innovation? You. Harvard Business Review.* https://hbr.org/2012/05/ whats-the-biggest-obstacle-to